Praise for SHERMAN BROWNE, *OVERCOMING DREAMICIDE,* and the AIMHIGH AMBASSADORS PROGRAM

"Professor Sherman Browne speaks to the soul of a person. He challenges the inner self to stand and become who you were called to be. He has the gift of empowerment and lives what he preaches and teaches. His perspective-shifting insights truly ignite your desire and catapult you into action."

—Kelly Dessin, Network Marketing Professional

"Some books will bring you value in the meantime, but there are others that will provide you with lessons for a lifetime. *Overcoming Dreamicide* is a lifetime book. These timeless principles, combined with the practical exercises and solutions are a Dreamers manual for success in business and life endeavors. Sherman Browne's timeless wisdom will help you exceed expectations!"

—Andre A. Samuels, Board Chairman, AIMHigh Empowerment Institute Inc.

"I proudly served for eight years in the U.S. Marine Corps. When I returned from Afghanistan my life was completely train wrecked. The things I saw and encountered were gruesome. When I signed up for courses with Sherman Browne, he sensed the sadness bottled up inside of me, but he also saw buried deep within me a "Great Leader". He poured new strength into me, resurrected my hope and redirected my focus. Today I am a better man because of what I learned from Sherman Browne."

—Kelvin Estevez, Ret. Sergeant U.S. Marine Corps

"Finally, a straight-forward, practical guide to conquering your dreams without the fluff that is traditionally offered from most self-help books. From the moment I opened the book, I was captivated by the stories, strategies, and systems that were provided. *Overcoming Dreamicide* is a game-changer for how to think, act and measure your progress!"

—Patrice Francois, Asst. Branch Manager
Ridgewood Savings Bank

"Rarely do you find someone who possesses such a potent gift for inspiration, who has the ability to unapologetically confront you on your non-sense (excuses), while simultaneously keeping you motivated to accomplish your goals. That is what you get from Sherman Browne and the AIMHigh Ambassadors program; they give you the pill that is often hard to swallow but is undoubtedly good for your personal and professional well-being. AIMHIGH IS THE REAL DEAL!"

—Moriah Cody, Youth and Young Adult Advocate

"POWERFUL, INSIGHTFUL, TRUTHFUL, AND PRACTICAL are the words to describe *Overcoming Dreamicide*. Sherman Browne's approach will certainly leave an indelible mark on your mind and in your life. Follow the steps of the systems provided and you'll experience joy and happiness in the pursuit of your dreams."

—Crystal Camejo, Graduate Student

OVERCOMING DREAMICIDE

» » » « « «

The Mindset, Methods and Metrics to
Execute Ideas and Keep Your Dreams Alive

To: Yury

Thank you for your support!!!.
Let's take your business to the
top.   #LiveyourDream

SHERMAN BROWNE

Editor: Yvette Hutchinson Powell
Cover and Interior Design: Joan Olson

Printed in the United States of America

Library of Congress Control Number: 2017918819
AIMHigh International, LLC, Bronx, NY

ISBN 978-0-9996974-0-5 (pbk)

ISBN 978-0-9996974-1-2 (ebook)

» » » « « «

*To Almighty God, thank you for the Gift of Life, and
for the calling you've laid on my heart to empower
your people. All Glory is unto Your Name.*

*To my wife, **Shereece**, and our beautiful daughter, **Solaei**.
Having you both in my life makes every day worth living.
Words can't express what your love means to me. I am
thankful for the very lineage that produced my
soul's counterpart and for the legacy that we
are now establishing together as a family.*

*To my parents, **Tracey and Irick Browne**, and **Dwyght,
Malika, and Shyar**. You are the foundation
of support that has been my compass
through unchartered territories.*

I dedicate this book to you.

» » » « « «

The poorest man in the world is the man without a dream. The most frustrated man in the world is the man with a dream that never becomes reality.

—Dr. Myles Munroe

CONTENTS

FOREWORD

Overcoming Dreamicide is well written, architecturally crafted, eloquent, and sophisticated. It begins with the author's mindset, the purpose to write, the ability to inspire hope, and the aptitude to make his intent practical. With over ten thousand hours served, hundreds of speeches delivered, and countless students mentored, Sherman Browne brings to life a unique set of methods and metrics, created through the experiences of world-class performers. This book will undoubtedly help ordinary people achieve extraordinary results.

Sherman delivers provocative insights that transcend generations. The journey, from his humble beginnings in the Caribbean, to gracing stages as a game-changing empowerment speaker, professor, entrepreneur, and author demonstrate what can happen when a common man exercises uncommon resilience. His upbringing and life experiences in business, government, nonprofit organizations, higher education, and faith-based settings have well equipped him, as he continues to practice what he teaches.

Sherman's perspective has transformed lives and allows people to peek into the soul of a man who is gifted through his ability to understand concepts that are not seen by the natural eye. Sherman has a vision beyond sight, which helps to unravel the complexities of life's challenges. His vision transports readers on paths to find the best in themselves.

The book raises questions over which many have pondered for generations: Why not me? Why can't I get ahead? If I have failed repeatedly, should I give up on my dreams? *Overcoming Dreamicide* provides the practical approach needed to suppress negative thinking that leads to the death of one's dream. This is truly a step-by-step guide to transform your mindset, behaviors, and habits.

Sherman Browne is a Dream Practitioner, and his wisdom makes this book a road map for success. It's a must read for dreamers, a toolkit for believers, and a manifesto for life-changers. Read, absorb, and apply, your life will forever be changed!

DR. CECIL D. WRIGHT
Author, *Twenty-One Days to Freedom*

INTRODUCTION

Hope deferred makes the heart sick, but
a longing fulfilled is a tree of life.
—PROVERBS 13:12

Her first words to me were "I used to know God by knowledge, but today, I know him by Faith."

It was September 2014 when I first met Miriam Edwards, a student at the college where I served as an adjunct professor. As Miriam cautiously rolled through the hallway in her wheelchair, my good friend, the Dean of Admissions, said to me, "Professor Browne, please share some encouraging words with this woman." When she introduced herself, I could hear the deep-rooted trepidation in her voice, as she was about to take this new journey in pursuit of higher education. It wasn't easy for Miriam to be there, especially after what she had been through four years prior.

Optimists often say, "Today is the first day of the rest of your life"—a truism, except for the day a person dies. September 18, 2010, could have been that day for Miriam, but the Lord (destiny) had different plans for her.

It was the day after her birthday. Miriam, along with thirteen members of her church, travelled in a van from the borough of the Bronx to Schenectady, New York to attend a banquet. Suddenly, as reported by the *New York Daily News*, the rear left tire exploded, flipping and rolling the van several times, killing six passengers on the scene, and another dying shortly thereafter.

As for Miriam, she was ejected from the vehicle, dragged along the road, and found submerged in a pool of her own blood. To this day, she still has no recollection of the accident due to the traumatic brain and head injuries she suffered.

She was immediately airlifted to Jacobi Medical Center and was in a coma for six days after sustaining numerous life threatening injuries. Her back was broken; both hips dislocated; shoulders jolted; her face scarred, marred, and disfigured; neck fractured, as well as having her left femur shattered. Miriam also had a broken patella and a fractured orbital in her left eye. It was devastating. Many, including some of her doctors, admitted being pessimistic about her potential for recovery. Family members in her native country of Jamaica started planning her funeral, but Miriam did not die.

Doctors considered amputating her left leg due to a lack of blood circulation but later opted for a skin graph procedure. Miriam spent three months in the surgical intensive care unit and burn center, subsequently enduring more than twelve reconstructive surgeries. She was later transferred to another hospital for rehabilitation, where she spent six weeks. This was followed by months of outpatient therapy.

After everything transpired, doctors told Miriam that she would be confined to a wheelchair for the rest of her life. What they didn't know was that Miriam had already decided that her near-death experience would not translate to a death sentence for her dreams. Miriam exceeded the doctors' expectations, motivated herself against all odds, and decided that she would eventually retire the wheelchair. The process was not easy. Miriam experienced moments of uncertainty, days of excruciating pain, months of hopelessness, years of indecisiveness, and extended periods of drowning in self-pity. But somewhere in all of her dilemma, she envisioned a silver lining of hope and consoled herself with the old adage, "What doesn't kill you makes you stronger." After four years of living in fear of the unknown, Miriam decided to move forward with her dream of attending college and arrived on that day in her wheelchair, ready to begin.

When I heard Miriam's story, I looked at her square in the eyes and said, "My dear, you don't need any words of encouragement from me. You are a modern day miracle, and when you graduate from college, your story of hope will literally inspire the world."

She responded, "Sir, you have no clue how your words have just spoken life into my dead situation, faith into my fears, and hope to my sobbing heart." It was the beginning of our journey together.

Today, Miriam's left leg is held together with steel and surgical wires, but with limited functional capacity. She completed three courses with me. Although she entered the college in September 2014 in a wheelchair, in June 2017 Miriam walked across the stage on her own feet for her graduation at Madison Square Garden. She graduated with a 4.0 grade point average, earned summa cum laude honors, and received a bachelor's degree in criminal justice, which I renamed, "the bachelor's degree in hope". After limping across the stage with less than perfect strides, Miriam descended cautiously down the stairs. I looked on with great pride to be associated with this woman who showed us by example how to keep our dreams alive. I asked her, "How do you feel Miriam?"

She responded "Professor Browne, this moment is priceless. Every step I take overwhelms me with uncontrollable joy. My eyelids can't withstand the fountain of tears that flood down my cheeks. At this moment, divinity has kissed humanity, and I hear the voice of God saying, 'I am well pleased.'" Miriam's journey was a hope fulfilled, a goal realized—a dream kept alive. Ms. Miriam Edwards is the epitome of what it means to Overcome Dreamicide!

Hopes and Dreams

They say you can live for forty days without food, three days without water, and eight minutes without air, but not one second without hope. Why? Because hope fulfills the human need to look toward something promising. I once read that the key to happiness in life is having something to do, something to love, and something to hope for. Hope is the gateway to your dreams. In this context, I'm not referring to the dreams you experience in your sleep, but, rather, the inspiring and empowering vision that invents your future. Your dreams are *"the sparks of possibility buried in your soul, which ignite your innovative and creative powers toward the pursuit of your purpose."*

We all have dreams. Some are personal or professional, while others might be social, financial, academic, or spiritual. These dreams are the aspirations we hope to make real; they give us a sense of purpose. So here's the question: When you've lost hope in your dreams, when you can't determine how to make them a reality, what should you do?

Unfortunately, rather than pushing through obstacles and persevering, many choose to ignore their dreams, or they give up on them altogether, until eventually it dies. In short, they commit Dreamicide.

Dreamicide Defined

The suffix "-cide" is a Latin term meaning "killer," or "the act of killing". It is often used in the formation of compound words (i.e. suicide, homicide, genocide). For the purpose of this book, the term "Dreamicide" is used to describe when a person either intentionally, or unintentionally kills his or her own dream. There's no attempt to resuscitate the dream, because the person is either unaware that the dream is dying, or they lack the inspiration to take action. When someone commits Dreamicide, often there is no explanation; there is no hidden letter that explains the motive. We seldom know why individuals become victims of Dreamicide. Across the board, Dreamicide has disastrous results. The person goes on living an unfulfilled life, and deprives the world of what could have been an amazing contribution to society. All because he or she either lost hope or neglected to take the necessary actions to keep their dreams alive.

Ask yourself, if you were to stand before a judge and jury today, would you be found guilty of committing Dreamicide? Are you currently living life below your potential, all because you've been stifling your dream? Do you have ideas that you just can't seem to get off the ground? Do you earnestly want improvements in specific areas of your life? If this sounds like you, I have good news. By choosing to read this book, you are taking the first step toward resurrecting your dreams. And you're not alone. As your "dream advocate," I'm here to help give your dream the life it deserves. Together, we will beat this case.

There are two reasons for most of our problems in life: we either act without thinking, or we keep thinking without acting. I think the latter holds the most truth. Too often, we think about what we want to do, we fantasize about it, but fail to take action. As you read this book, the first point to ponder is this: *an ounce of action weighs more than a ton of intentions.* Simply put, you will gain much more from this book if you start taking the necessary steps to live your dream, rather than just thinking about what you one day intend to do. Actions speak louder than intentions and goals.

Now, let's be clear, living your dream will require the retraining of your mind. Someone who has been in a coma over an extended period of time has to go through physical therapy to re-acclimate to his or her own body. Your dream may have been in a coma, but it's not dead. Step-by-step, we will walk together through this process.

So, Sherman, why this book?

This book will positively shift your thinking. It will help you to progressively implement ideas, improve results, and accomplish personal dreams that lead to a more fulfilled life.

Today, I believe we're facing a crisis of personal confidence, one in which people have stopped believing in themselves and have become comfortable settling for mediocrity. This has led to a life of self-sabotaging misery. People are spending too much time comparing social media statuses, making too many efforts to impress others by pretending like they have it all together. People are spending countless hours drowning in self-pity, because the grass looks greener on the other side. Well guess what? The grass is greener, but the water bill is also much higher. If you begin to focus on watering *your* grass, you will experience your own greener pastures. Take care of your lawn, and stop lurking at your neighbor's property. Especially, when your grass (your dream) is dying. Dreamicide is an epidemic, and this book is the intervention.

Over my years of speaking to audiences; working as an adjunct professor; and serving thousands of people in the public, private, and nonprofit sectors, what I've repeatedly encountered are individuals searching for ways to execute the ideas and dreams that reside in their hearts and minds. So I've read other books, attended conferences, and asked probing questions. The traditional recommendations are philosophies and principles that should be adopted to make your dreams a reality. We get the WHY and the WHAT, but seldom do we get the HOW. *Overcoming Dreamicide* is designed to provide all three. Every chapter gives you the philosophies and principles to follow, but it also provides practical steps to make it happen.

Don't just read this book, interact with it, internalize the stories, and answer the reflective questions for yourself. Every chapter ends with summary takeaways and next steps to move you further along your journey.

The Structure

This book is broken down into three sections—Mindset, Methods, and Metrics.

MINDSET: At the outset, we'll be focusing on your mindset. This is where the most important work must be done. Before anything great is accomplished physically, it must first be accomplished mentally. Your mindset will determine your will-set—your will and determination to overcome Dreamicide. *Overcomers believe that your mindset is of utmost importance, because what you do and who you are is a result of how you think.*

METHODS: Next we'll focus on your methods. These are the specific sequence of steps and actions utilized to keep dreams alive. People often get stuck because they are clueless about what to do next; they become confused—and confused people do nothing. Here you will find practical strategies that have been proven by the most elite overcomers of Dreamicide. *Overcomers are confident that adopting best practices highly increases the probability of achieving a desired outcome.*

METRICS: Lastly, we will develop and focus on effective metrics. This is how you will measure your results. It's natural to feel like giving up when you don't immediately see the fruits of your labor, but here you will gain a new perspective on how to track and focus on what matters most on the journey toward your dreams. *Overcomers understand that the true measure of success is progress. But progress is a process that must be appreciated before you are elevated.*

All Rise!

It was Zig Ziglar, the great motivational speaker, who said, "You don't have to be great to get started, but you have to get started to become great." Today, as you read this book, you are taking action by choosing to enrich your mind and discover the tools and techniques to live your dreams. But, like anything else in life, reading without applying the information will do nothing but make you a dream-scholar with an in-depth understanding of Dream Living strategies. It will not make you a dream-practitioner; my hope is that you choose to be a practitioner. Let today be the day that your dead dreams are resurrected, or that your sleeping dreams are awakened. This is the moment we've all been waiting for.

Judge: In the case of *(YOUR NAME) VS. THE STATE OF YOUR DREAMS*, on the count of Dreamicide in the first degree, how does the Jury find the Defendant?

Jury: Your Honor, we find the Defendant (YOUR NAME), NOT GUILTY.

Today is the day of your acquittal!

SECTION I

mindset

mīn(d)set/

noun

A mental attitude or disposition that predetermines a person's responses to and interpretations of situations.

THE OVERCOMERS MINDSET

Overcomers of Dreamicide understand that everything begins with your mindset; it is the nucleus of your dream. Your mindset serves as your compass giving you guidance in the midst of unchartered territories. Overcomers don't believe that their mindset is fixed; they believe that success character traits such as being intelligent, empathetic, hardworking, and resourceful are something you become, not something you're born with. Overcomers have a growth mindset.

LIVING TO DIE:
THE CLOCK IS TICKING

Every man dies. Not every man lives.

—WILLIAM WALLACE
AS QUOTED IN *Braveheart*

You have made my days a mere handbreadth;
the span of my years is as nothing before
you. Everyone is but a breath, even
those who seem secure.

PSALM 39:5 NIV

October 25, 2011. As I walked through the halls of Mount Sinai Hospital, I couldn't help but reflect on the incredible lesson I had just learned from my grandmother—Jennifer Stanley. Little did I know, my departure on that day would be the last time I'd say goodbye to her. After a short sixty-nine years on earth, her expiration was imminent, as she suffered from severe cirrhosis of the liver.

Emotions were high as her husband, children, extended family, and friends waited in heart-wrenching anticipation for what the doctors said was inevitable—her death. I reflected on my earlier journey to New York City and how she had allowed me to reside with her until I became financially stable. I remembered all the nights she scolded me about the importance of washing the dishes before going to bed and how I should never go to sleep with a dirty house. But of all the lessons she taught me, her final one while on her deathbed resonated the most.

During her last few days, she repeatedly mentioned all the things she could have, should have, and would have done if she had more time. She spoke of all the tasks that she failed to complete, and the dreams she wished were fulfilled. My grandmother expressed concern for what was going to happen to her family and whether or not we would be able to survive financially, socially, and emotionally without her presence. My grandmother questioned whether she adequately established a strong foundation for us to develop from. On that day she taught me an incredible lesson; I learned from my dying grandmother that *most people don't attempt to live until they're about to die.*

You Will Expire

Jennifer, as she was affectionately known, was loving, caring, kind-hearted, selfless, and extremely entertaining. You could never visit her home and leave empty-handed. She always made sure that you departed with something of value. During the six years that I lived with her, two characteristics that stuck with me were her unwavering commitment to her job and her relentless work ethic. For over thirty-five years, she worked diligently as a home health aide, doing everything in her power to make an honest living, but in the end I wondered, was she honestly living? You may be wondering why I asked. Well, let's examine this together.

My grandmother knew how to enjoy herself and was always full of exuberance when attending family gatherings. But she spent the majority of her time working hard on the job for countless hours to maintain her household. It made me wonder, with all her talents, abilities, gifts, and skills, were there more goals that she could have accomplished? Did the world get to fully experience this talented, gifted, and cheerful woman? Did she give life to her greatest dreams? I wondered because, of all the things she wished to have accomplished, I never heard her mention the desire to have worked more hours on her job. Yet, that's where she spent the majority of her time. Ponder this thought for a moment: it's possible that you could spend your entire life making an honest living, without HONESTLY LIVING. *Overcomers of Dreamicide always ask themselves, Am I Honestly Living? Am I living life on my terms? Am I doing the things that I truly care deeply about?* If the answers to these questions are not unequivocally YES, then adjustments are immediately required.

As you delve into this chapter, let's be clear. The purpose is not to dampen your spirit; it's only intended to provide perspective. To put it plainly, you should know that your aspiration has an expiration. Everyone has dreams they hope to accomplish, but as you go through life, it's easy to postpone the pursuit of those dreams for another day, week, month, or year. You're in full control of that decision. But the one thing you cannot postpone is the day of your death. Last night someone died; this morning someone died. And even as you're reading this chapter, YOU ARE DYING. Your life clock is always ticking, so while you choose to postpone your dream for a future date, just remember, that future date is not guaranteed. There will be a time when it's just too late to accomplish what you intended. My grandmother realized this fact and encouraged me, before she died, to continue making progress related to my faith, family, fitness, finances, and fulfillment. This epiphany was not unique to my grandmother; it has been a common revelation among the elderly for centuries.

The Regret of Wasted Worries

In 2004, Dr. Karl Pillemer, Professor in the Department of Human Development at Cornell University conducted a study of more than 1,500 elderly Americans over the age of sixty-five. The purpose of his study was to uncover what tried and true advice he could gain from the wisest Americans. Surprisingly, while he learned much about their insights related to careers, relationships, parenting, and education, one of the most salient lessons he learned was that many of the respondents suffered from what I call "The Regret of Wasted Worries." During his study, Dr. Pillemer repeatedly heard expressions of regret from these elderly participants about the time they spent worrying. One respondent put it this way: "I poisoned my life by worrying obsessively, even though I had no control of what would happen." During one interview, Dr. Pillemer was asked, what was the greatest insight he gained from his study? He replied, "Live like your life is short." This is indeed profound advice.

Looking at this study, I'm reminded that while we are aspiring, we are also expiring. Worrying and waiting, therefore, is a zero-value proposition. *The longer you take to live your dream, the less time you will have to enjoy it.* So, what are your worries? Are you worried that your idea might not work? Are you worried that you could potentially fail? Are you worried that people will speak unfavorably of your attempt? Look, I get it. All of these potential scenarios are valid, but on the other hand, what is worrying doing for you? That's right—absolutely nothing. You'll never be fulfilled by your worries; your financial institution will never accept worries as deposits into your bank account, and worrying will never feed your children. Overcomers of Dreamicide understand that worrying has no value—it's an inexcusable waste of time.

Often, I begin my presentations by quoting American

humorist Art Buchwald, who said, "Whether it's the best of times or the worst of times, it's the only time we've got." I use this thought-provoking perspective to remind my audience about the brevity of life. Whether you consider this moment to be good or bad, the countdown to your demise has already begun. Waiting and worrying about potential setbacks will not add value to your life. My favorite book asks the question in this way, "Can any one of you by worrying add a single hour to your life?" (Matthew 6:27 NIV). Whenever I reflect on this verse in the Bible, I am encouraged to quit worrying and just start DOING.

The YOLO Mindset

The term YOLO (You Only Live Once) was popularized in 2011, when recording artist Drake introduced the song "The Motto." The phrase is used to express that one should enjoy life to the fullest, as if there won't be another chance for it. I can only imagine how many dreams would be alive today if this mindset was embraced more broadly.

Time is the most sacred of all commodities. It can never be replaced, replenished, or restored. Every moment not used to live your dreams is a moment lost that you'll never regain. Recognizing this fact, it's important that you pursue your calling without hesitation. Unfortunately, many find themselves complaining about past experiences or focusing so much on future goals that they neglect taking present action.

I came across a great illustration of this point when I read an article where the Dalai Lama was asked, what surprises him most about humanity? His response was "Man. Because man sacrifices his health in order to make money. Then he sacrifices money to recuperate his health. And then man is so anxious about the future that he does not enjoy the present; the result being that he does not live in the present or the future; he lives as if he is never going to die, and then dies having never really lived." To overcome Dreamicide, it's imperative to embrace the YOLO mindset. If you only live once, you have nothing to lose by making the best of it.

Everyday spent not living your dream is another "Dead Day" on earth. A poet once argued that most men are dead by the age of twenty-five but are just waiting to be buried. The metaphor is intended to point out that people die at the moment they stop pursuing their dream and are simply awaiting their traditional funeral. In life, the clock is always ticking—there is no such thing as dead time. All that exists is the amount of time one spends living dead or being fully alive. How much time are you spending living dead? Waiting is a dead act; worrying about circumstances is a dead act; complaining is a dead act. *How much longer will you choose to be the living dead?*

The One-Minute Life

I remember listening to legendary TV host, Larry King, as he interviewed Dr. Neil deGrasse Tyson, the renowned astrophysicist and science communicator. During the interview, these two powerful men had one of the most fascinating exchanges on the topic of the afterlife. The question was asked, If you could live forever, would you? To which Larry King immediately answered, "Yes." On the other hand, Dr. deGrasse Tyson had a rather enlightening perspective. He said, "It is the knowledge that I'm going to die that creates the focus that I bring to being alive. The urgency of accomplishment, the need to express love *now*, not later. If we live forever, why ever even get out of bed in the morning—because you always have tomorrow? That's not the type of life I want to lead." Hearing Dr. deGrasse Tyson's response was profound but also puzzling. Just to think that a man would prefer to know that he is going to die rather than have the chance to live forever. But I completely understood his point of view. In that very moment, I recognized *the brevity of life creates the urgency in life—the urgency to live fully now*. So what would life be like if you were maximizing every single minute? What would you do, where would you go, and who would you become in that very minute?

The most important daily decision we make is how to use our limited time. Dr. Benjamin Elijah Mays summed it up best when he quoted the following anonymous poem.

"God's Minute"

I have only a minute
Only sixty seconds in it.
Forced upon me,
Can't refuse it,
Didn't seek it,
Didn't choose it
But it's up to me to use it.
I must suffer if I lose it
Give account if I abuse it
Just a tiny little minute
But eternity is in it.

Imagine for a moment that you only had "a tiny little minute" to live. What would you do if you could accomplish anything you wanted? Well, the clever action to take in this scenario would probably be to ask for more time. Ideally, if this was a fairy tale, you might be able to get that wish granted. But since this is not a fairy tale, we are unable to ask for more time. We could make more money, acquire more things, buy bigger houses, yachts and cars, but we can't earn more time. I've come across countless students, friends, family members, and colleagues who have forgotten how essential it is to use time wisely. Many have reached the point that they've allowed their time to be dictated by nonessential matters. *I too, once focused so much on the job for which I got paid, while neglecting the calling for which I was made.* Now, don't misunderstand my point; there are certain activities that you must always endure for the time being to make ends meet, but you should never allow those tasks to become what you do for your lifetime. If you've made a commitment to any activity that is not a deeply ingrained passion of yours, if your vocation is not connected to your purpose, then you need to start coordinating your exit strategy.

Your Dream vs. Your Job

Life is so miserable when your limited time is spent building other people's dream at the expense of your own. When your dream is alive, you will find passion, purpose, pleasure, power, profits, and ultimately Peace of Mind. Peace of Mind is impossible to have without discovering, pursuing, and living on passion and purpose. A lack of Peace of Mind is what causes the customer care representative to display a negative attitude—all because you asked additional questions. A lack of Peace of Mind is what causes the waitress to rudely cut you off midsentence because you changed your mind about your order. When a person lacks peace of mind, it is usually the result of a misalignment between their purpose and their current situation. The countdown has begun, and time is running out. Stop waiting to start living the life you've envisioned; you have nothing to lose but time.

Years from now you're going to wish you started today. One way to hold yourself accountable to the best use of your time is to ask yourself, *Will the YOU, five years from now, thank the present YOU for the way you are currently using your time?* Reduce the amount of countless hours scrolling down your social media feed, reduce the time you spend gossiping, or discussing matters that are not conducive to your growth. Begin using your time wisely, because the future YOU is depending on the present use of your time. Stop waiting, worrying, and complaining and start living, doing, and achieving. The countdown has already begun; there is no better time than NOW!

SUMMARY TAKEAWAYS

Your Aspiration has an Expiration

» At some point we will all expire. To live before you die means to take action while you have the ability to do so. The longer you take to live your dream, the less time you'll have to enjoy it.

Worrying has no value

» Excessive worry causes dream paralysis. Your worries may be legitimate, but what's on the other side of worry? NOTHING. Even when you feel worried, I would suggest you still take action. You have nothing to lose but time.

Your dream vs. your job

» Your job is what you get paid for, but your calling is what you were made for. If your job aligns with your dream, then stick with it, but if not, you need to strategize about your transition.

WHAT'S NEXT?

» In the table provided, list three of your current aspirations or areas you wish to improve. For each one, name and write the worries or concerns that have paralyzed your progress. Now that we're aware of what worries and concerns you, determine what these apprehensions are doing for you. Once you recognize that your mindless worries are not adding value, write the actions you will take immediately within 24–48 hours to get moving on making those aspirations and improvements happen.

YOUR ASPIRATIONS	YOUR WORRIES/ CONCERNS	YOUR IMMEDIATE ACTIONS
1.		
2.		
3.		

TAKING RISKS: CHOOSING COURAGE OVER COMFORT

You can choose courage or you can choose comfort, but you cannot choose both.

—BRENE BROWN

Have I not commanded you? Be strong and courageous. Do not be afraid; do not be discouraged, for the Lord your God will be with you wherever you go. "

JOSHUA 1:9 NIV

Over my seven years of serving as an adjunct professor of criminal justice, I've developed a profound respect for our men and women in uniform. Whether they serve in the military, law enforcement, emergency management services, or our fire departments, we owe first responders a debt of gratitude. Just think of the selfless sacrifice these individuals make every day to keep our communities and cities safe.

In the summer of 2016, I had the pleasure of addressing over five hundred cadets of the New York City Police Department, the largest police force in the United States. The cadets are aspiring officers who receive training necessary to serve on the police force. At one point during my remarks, I asked a simple, but profound question. "Why are you here?" As I randomly selected cadets to answer the question, I heard time and again, "I want to be a police officer." After hearing this response, I expressed to the cadets that I couldn't accept their answer. It just did not make sense. Standing before me were over five hundred men and women who were voluntarily choosing to run toward danger on a daily basis. I thought of days such as September 11, 2001, when nineteen terrorists attacked the United States of America by flying airplanes into the World Trade Center in New York City and the Pentagon, and were foiled in a fourth attempt, possibly on the White House. While thousands of civilians were running away from the chaos, our first responders were running toward it. The mere thought of running toward danger just seemed too irrational for me. So again, I asked. "Why are you here?" Upon further discussion, many of the cadets shared their personal stories and experiences that led them to serve. Some lost family members to horrific crimes that were never solved; others felt compelled to carry on their families' legacies of serving as police officers. Yet, many expressed that it was necessary to serve in honor of the first responders who had already sacrificed their lives on September 11. *The factor that distinguishes our first responders from many others is that while most people would choose to F.E.A.R. (Forget Everything And Run), these first responders choose to turn fear around and do the unthinkable, which is to F.E.A.R. (Face Everything And Rise).* Our first responders demonstrate to us every day what it means to choose courage over comfort.

Courage over Comfort

Overcoming Dreamicide will require that you intake high dosages of discomfort. You must determine whether or not you're willing to sacrifice your comfort for your growth. Just like a child receives periodic vaccinations to reduce the risks of specific illnesses, enduring discomfort is the required vaccination to keep your dreams alive.

Take a moment and reflect on the things that we use the most in our daily lives: computers, tablets, cell phones, light bulbs, automobiles, and airplanes. Many of these inventions were once only a figment of the world's imagination. How did they get here? Where did they come from? Who thought of these brilliant ideas? More importantly, how did these dreams become reality?

It begs the question: How is it that some dreams live abundant lives, while others meet their tragic demise? The answer depends on whether or not you have the courage to take risks and sacrifice comfort. Some of the world's greatest innovations were developed as a result of dreamers who were willing to take risks. Although there was no way to absolutely guarantee that these inventions would be successful, the dreamers took the risk of moving forward regardless of the possibility of failure. On their journey, some were told that their ideas were impossible, that their dreams were too far-fetched and that they would never garner support for their vision. Many were told to stick to what they already knew. Yet, even after all of the cynicism and criticism, these individuals still brought to life some of the greatest innovations and have shifted our mindset as to what is possible.

So how do you know whether you've chosen courage over comfort or vice versa? To answer this question, you must engage in a thorough self-evaluation to determine whether your thoughts, actions, and habits are comfortably killing your dreams or giving your dreams the life they deserve. President John F. Kennedy once said, "There are risks and costs to a program of action. But they are far less than the long-range risks and costs of comfortable inaction." If you want your dreams to live, you must become a risk taker now.

No Risk, No Reward

Speaking from experience, I can attest that the decision to take a risk is quite challenging. It requires you to suppress the feelings of doubt, fear, skepticism, and uncertainty that will dominate your thoughts. Although these feelings of anxiety are real, the rewards to be gained are also real. *Without risks, life becomes a set of routine activities that lead to predictable outcomes.* Imagine always knowing how everything will turn out. What incentives would you have to explore new ideas? Absolutely none. Everything you do would become boring and monotonous.

Risks are only worth taking because of the potential rewards that could be gained as a result of venturing into the unknown. While we need certainty in life, it is our need for uncertainty that drives our pursuits. Uncertainty makes us feel alive; it gives us variety and breaks us out of patterns. People engage in skydiving, bungee jumping, zip lining, and mountain climbing for the thrill and for the opportunity to prove that they can go beyond perceived limits. The fulfillment gained from accomplishing the goal makes the risk worth taking. This confirms the old adage, "No risk, no reward."

Should I Stay, or Should I Go?

I was raised in the beautiful paradise of the U.S. Virgin Islands (USVI)—a territory of the United States composed of four small islands—St. Thomas, St. John, St. Croix, and Water Island. It's the place where the values of manners and respect were woven into the fabric of my character. These islands are the birthplace of world-class achievers like five-time NBA champion Tim Duncan, Grammy nominated singer/songwriter duo RCity, and international reggae sensation Pressure Busspipe. Beyond the islands' beautiful people and culture, the USVI is known for its white-sand beaches, coral reefs, and verdant hills. It's a place that you should visit at least once in your lifetime. This place, where people from all across the globe, travel for thousands of miles to visit for vacation, is where I was fortunate to call home. Now, you can understand the magnitude of my dilemma: Should I stay, or should I go?

When I graduated from Ivanna Eudora Kean High School, I remember being faced with this major decision. Do I stay in the beautiful island paradise where I am comfortable, fairly well known, and secure, or do I leave for New York City to pursue my dreams of becoming a hip-hop choreographer and dancehall reggae performer? I promise you, I was a great performer. I just knew in my heart that I would one day be gracing the world's biggest stages. It was only after a few attempts and doors being closed that I realized I wasn't really cut out for the industry. I was more intrigued by the perceived perks of superstar status but didn't want to go through the process that superstars endured. Okay, I confess: I killed my own dream of becoming a dancehall reggae superstar.

Anyway, let me get back to my dilemma. Obviously, when weighing these options, it would've been easier to stick to what I knew, but that would have steered me to ultimate boredom. Eventually, I decided to take the leap of faith, and with only four hundred dollars in my savings account, I decided to take a bite of the Big Apple.

Now, if you know anything about New York City, the cost of

living is very high; therefore, four hundred dollars was sure to run out in the blink of an eye. For me, that "blink" happened rather quickly. Between shopping for the latest designer clothing and paying hundreds of dollars for cell phone charges after exceeding the minutes in my data plan, I was totally broke in less than a month. Here I was, at the age of nineteen in this big city without money, a job, or plan for my life. My initial thought was to call my mother and return to the US Virgin Islands; I also contemplated moving to Massachusetts where my father was living at the time. But for me, both options would have left me embarrassed, particularly because I always boasted and declared that I could make it on my own. What made matters worse was the fact that my living conditions in New York were totally contrary to what I envisioned.

From the USVI to New York State

As a young man, I grew up in very humble circumstances. My living conditions were in no way extravagant, but the enormous deposits of love from my parents cancelled out any potential indication in my mind that we were living in poverty. My mother, Tracey Browne, raised both my brother and me on a yearly salary of $11,000 (USD). I never thought it was odd that the kitchen was also our living room and bedroom. I never thought it was problematic that on some days we only had sliced bread, water from the faucet, and ramen noodles in the cupboard. I remember the days when I would pour water on the white sliced bread to increase the weight of the bread in hopes of feeling the sensation that I ate a full meal. During that time, I actually thought we were receiving great nutritional value. Never did I believe my conditions were poor, because I had nothing with which to compare my reality. But with the Virgin Islands being my point of reference, I must admit, my expectations for New York City were a bit extravagant. I thought the streets would be paved with gold and money would grow from the trees. I envisioned myself living like a king. My assumption was that anyone living abroad had to be rich. Nothing was further from the truth.

When I arrived in New York City, I moved to the Bronx, the birthplace of hip-hop. I was totally unaware that the neighborhood where I resided had the distinction of being the poorest congressional district in the United States. *Yes, I said it—the poorest congressional district in the United States of America.* So when I arrived, there were conditions for which I was totally unprepared. I wasn't used to being in twenty-degree weather without heat or hot water in the apartment. I couldn't understand why the neighbors played the music so loudly from sundown to sunrise. It was perplexing that people thought it was acceptable to urinate in the hallways. And for the life of me, I couldn't understand why there was such a large infestation of roaches and rats in our building. The rodents were like living with neighbors; I felt as if I was the one disrupting their quality of life. I share all of this to point out that not only was it uncomfortable for me to leave the U.S. Virgin Islands, but it quickly became uncomfortable to live in New York City. I had to make a decision. Do I travel back to the white-sand beaches in paradise or make it work in the concrete jungle? What should I do? What made matters worse was an encounter that I had with my friend Deidra, a childhood friend who grew up with me in the islands.

I encountered Deidra when I was walking through Fordham Road, a well-known shopping district in the Bronx. When I saw her, we were both excited and began catching up.

The Deidra Encounter

Deidra: Sherman, oh my god! How are you? It's so good to see you. I didn't know you were here in New York.

Me: Wow, it's great to see you too. I just moved here about a month ago. What have you been up to?

Deidra: Well, I'm in college working on my bachelor's degree and currently doing an internship. I more than likely will be hired. Everything is working out for me right now. Making a lot of progress. How about you?

Me: Huh . . . well . . . I mean . . . You know . . . I'm here working on my music and choreography. (This was a lie.) I'm possibly going to be doing a music video. (This was an even bigger lie.)

Deidra: Oh wow. What's the song, who's the artist, and when will the video be coming out?

Me: Well, we're not sure yet; it's still in the works. (Digging myself into a deeper hole with this lie.)

Deidra: Oh, okay. Well good luck with that. Let's exchange phone numbers and stay in touch.

Me: Well my phone is not working right now; I'm going to the store to get it fixed. Give me your number, and I'll be in touch with you. (Still lying, my phone was disconnected for lack of payment.)

Deidra: Okay. It was good seeing you.

Have you ever been in this type of scenario? I remember my encounter with Deidra as being one of the most embarrassing moments that I ever experienced. Here it was, I reconnected with a childhood friend and heard about how well she was doing, but I, on the other hand, had nothing of value to share for myself. When I reflected on this moment, I thought to myself, staying in New York could be risky, because I could end up failing miserably, but staying in New York could also be an opportunity to prove that I could make it in the Big Apple.

It has been said, "A ship in harbor is safe, but that is not what ships are built for." I had to decide whether to return to the safe harbor of the US Virgin Islands or to sail on the deep seas for my dreams. I chose the latter, and it was a defining moment of my life. What would have been the result of me staying in my comfort zone? What would I have forfeited by choosing comfort over courage? I guess we'll never know. The task always seems daunting and sometimes impossible until it is done. Babies turn over before they crawl, then crawl before they stand, they stand before they walk, and then walk before they run. Every step of the way, babies risk potentially hurting themselves, but taking the risk is necessary for their development. Overcomers of Dreamicide know that if you're eager for your dream to grow and live, you will be required to take risks. No one ever learned how to swim by standing on the beach. You have to jump into the water and begin paddling if you expect to swim.

The Danger of Comfort

Comfort is a beautiful and relaxing place, but nothing grows in comfort. Everything you really want in life is right outside of your comfort zone. To sacrifice comfort is an act of courage; that's why courage and comfort can't occupy the same space. You could choose to remain stagnant in the comfort of what you know or make progress by having the courage to grow. Your comfort zone is your broke zone; it's your unfulfilled zone. Your comfort zone will never be your growth, success, or "dreams made real" zone. I implore you to choose courage over comfort; it's the only way you'll overcome Dreamicide. "Rest in peace" (RIP) is used figuratively when someone dies, as a way to signify eternal comfort. Remaining in comfort while you're still alive means your dreams are resting in peace.

SUMMARY TAKEAWAYS

Your comfort must be sacrificed

» Your comfort has given you what you have. If you want more, you must do more than you've done. You will have to give up comfort for growth.

The risks are worth the rewards.

» The rewards of living your dream are worth every risk that you are going to take. The alternative is remaining where you are. Thriving will always be more exciting than merely surviving.

F.E.A.R.: Forget Everything And Run or Face Everything And Rise

» Fear can either destroy you or drive you. You can choose to remain in your comfort zone or decide to live in your dream zone. Feel the fear and do it anyway; that is the hallmark of choosing courage over comfort.

WHAT'S NEXT?

» To help you break out of your comfort zone it would be beneficial to periodically force yourself into uncomfortable scenarios. Your muscles of discomfort should be exercised repeatedly, until you get to the point where you are comfortable being uncomfortable.

» List three uncomfortable activities that are necessary for the furtherance of your dreams (e.g. public speaking, networking, sales, etc.) Beside each one, create a scenario that would force you to feel discomfort while engaged in the activity.

» Lastly, create an immediate plan of action to which you will commit yourself. Engaging in this uncomfortable activity will help you to exercise your muscles of discomfort.

UNCOMFORTABLE ACTIVITY	SCENARIO THAT CAUSES DISCOMFORT	IMMEDIATE ACTIONS
Ex. Public Speaking	Mandatory Weekly Presentations	Join Toastmasters
1.		
2.		
3.		

THE PAIN OF PROGRESS: POWER THROUGH THE PROCESS

"Pain is temporary. It may last for a minute, or
an hour or a day, or even a year. But eventually,
it will subside. And something else will take its
place. If I quit, however, it will last forever."

—LANCE ARMSTRONG

Take pains with these things; be absorbed in
them, so that everyone will see your progress.

1 TIMOTHY 4:15 NET

June 30, 2014, 10:54 p.m. I was in the midst of a conference call, when my wife ran into our home office and said, "We have to leave now; I can't take it anymore." In that very second I felt emotions of nervousness, anxiety, and excitement all at the same time. Over a period of forty weeks, I watched her body go through a metamorphosis as she endured the progressive feelings of fatigue and pain, natural occurrences during the development of the fetus in her womb. Shereece was pregnant, and her contractions were now recurring every five minutes, which was a sign that our princess was ready to make her royal entrance into the world.

We rushed to the hospital, and as we arrived, the security officer, who seemed to understand the reason for our frantic entrance, immediately volunteered to escort us to the labor and delivery unit. As the medical team connected the fetal monitoring system to Shereece, I couldn't help but reflect on the morning sickness, afternoon groans, and sleepless nights that she experienced at various stages of her pregnancy. It was perplexing to me that the more progress she made, the more pain she suffered, and now the culmination of this nine-month process was about to be realized.

Previously, Shereece and I had agreed that she would have an epidural, the most popular method of pain relief during labor, but she was already dilated at nine centimeters, which meant our baby was on her way. I remember the look on Shereece's face when the doctor informed us that she would have to forgo the epidural procedure, and deliver our child naturally. After all the pain she had already endured, she was about to endure even more. Shereece immediately cried and tried to negotiate, but the doctor said it was too late; he forewarned her that she was about to feel lots of pain but emphasized that she needed to *push through the pain* to expedite the process. Obviously, Shereece was not in the mood for any motivational rhetoric at the time, but that one line became my resounding mantra as I cheered her on through the process. "Push through the pain, hon; let's push through the pain . . ." to which she replied, "That's sure easy for you to say from the sidelines." The doctor and nurse looked at me, astonished, and said, "Dad sounds like a great coach." In between every push, Shereece would say, "I can't push any more." The mantra would be repeated again, "You're almost there, hon. Push through the pain . . ." Now, I've heard of women who endured active labor for two hours and even those who endured it for two days, but shockingly, it took Shereece only twenty minutes to deliver our nine-pound bundle of joy.

Yeah, that's right—nine pounds. I often say jokingly that my daughter's birth weight was a result of the oxtail and rice and peas that Shereece continually ate during her pregnancy. (She's Jamaican.) My wife's ability to push through the pain was the process that brought to life, in record time, our beautiful daughter, Solaei Raiel Browne!

The Price of Progress = Pain

It would be rational to think that as you make progress toward your dream, the process should become easier. Nothing is further from the truth. *Everything in life comes with a price, and the price of progress is pain.* The best way for me to illustrate this principle is by comparing your dream's process toward fruition to the stages of a woman's pregnancy. Now, for the gentlemen reading this, although we've never physically experienced active labor, I think there is much to learn from the stages that created our existence. For the ladies who've never been through pregnancy, this is a nonscientific explanation of what you might experience. The relevance of this process as it relates to your dreams is that your "dream" is your "unborn child", and you are "the mother" carrying the baby. So let's begin.

Stages of Pregnancy: the Stages of Your Dreams

A pregnancy goes through three stages, or trimesters. During these trimesters, there are experiences that both the mother and fetus will go through simultaneously. For the purposes of this metaphor, I will focus on the stages and experiences of the mother-to-be (you).

First Trimester: In the first trimester (1–12 weeks) a woman might be pregnant and not know it but will feel the symptoms due to hormonal changes happening in her body. It's similar to the discomfort you'll feel when you're "pregnant with your dream." Maybe you'll feel fatigue and uneasiness at your job or with the current state of affairs. It might be similar to the nausea and morning sickness that many women endure in the first trimester. It's a sign that something has changed. The mere smell of mediocrity becomes bothersome and makes you queasy. You will begin to wonder what's happening to you. Why do you feel such high levels of annoyance with your normal routines? You might start researching what these signs mean and then get a pregnancy test only to find that you are pregnant with your dream. Once you discover that you're pregnant, you will more than likely share the great news with a few of your closest friends and family. *Although there is nervousness when you discover that you're pregnant with a dream, there is also great excitement in anticipation for the fulfillment of that dream.*

Second Trimester: In the second trimester (13–27 weeks) the nausea and morning sickness may be reduced, but the fetus (your dream) is growing bigger, which causes a baby bump to appear. For most people on the outside it's cute, but to the person bearing the growth, there is more pregnancy weight being gained at the front of the body, which is also causing more back pain. The pain makes it slightly more difficult to accomplish daily tasks, such as walking, cooking, and working.

As it relates to your dream, the pain endured in the second trimester seems small, but it's more difficult to do your normal tasks while working on the dream simultaneously. Maybe people are telling you how proud they are of you for beginning something new or expanding on a venture, but they don't recognize the pain you're suffering, as you try to balance your dream with your previous and present priorities. Yes, you feel the back pain, but it's necessary because the dream is growing. For some, who can't take the pain, they might make the life-altering decision to abort the dream, recognizing that after week twenty-four, abortion is not an option. Your dream can't live if it's aborted. You are experiencing the common growing pains that many who are pregnant with a dream endure.

Third Trimester: In the third trimester (28–40 weeks), prepare for impact; the pain will be aggressive. At this stage, the woman's enlarged uterus pushes against the diaphragm; it becomes difficult to breathe due to the decreased room for her lungs to expand. Not only will the woman experience pain internally but the body will also begin to look drastically different. The ankles, hands, feet, and face may swell as she retains more fluids and her blood circulation slows. Her face may develop dark patches, and stretch marks may appear on her belly, thighs, breasts, and backside. It will become harder to find a comfortable sleeping position during the final weeks of pregnancy. Although this metamorphosis is occurring with the mother, the fetus is also fully developing. The mother is going through tremendous pain, but she is drawing nearer to delivery. One process can't happen without the other. The "Pain" and the "Progress" occur simultaneously, and so it will be as you're pursuing your dream. As you are drawing nearer to giving birth, you will find yourself working harder than ever before. Late nights will be the norm. At times you will be sleep deprived. In addition, you may oftentimes feel overwhelmed by the process. *Just like pain is necessary to give birth to a human life, it will be necessary for the birth and progression of your dream.*

So Sherman, what is the point of this entire metaphor? Well, I'm glad you asked. My point is simple: While the birth of a baby is amazing and beautiful, the process before the birth is unequivocally painful. You can't have one without the other. If you want your dreams to make progress, you must be ready, willing, and able to endure the painful process.

The Pain of Progress

To make the kind of progress that will enable you to overcome Dreamicide, you will have to endure painful experiences. A writer once said, "If you're not willing to sacrifice for what you want, then what you want will eventually become your sacrifice." What often hinders people from realizing their dream is their unwillingness to sacrifice unhealthy habits, while embracing the necessary growing pains. If you intend to overcome Dreamicide, you cannot expect to continue with the same habits, traits, and activities. It's insane for anyone to think that they could do the same thing but get a different result. Remember, what you've done has given you what you have, and if you're not living your dreams, then you must try something different. *Sacrifice is painful, but necessary for progress—you develop power through the process.* So what are the pains that you will undergo in pursuit of your dreams? Just like you have three stages of pregnancy, I submit to you three stages of pain you will experience when giving birth to your dreams.

The Pain of Rejection

Rejection is one of the toughest pains you will ever have to tolerate. And it's painful because of one word: NO.

The word NO is one of the most powerful words in the English language. It only has two letters, but this small word has the power to leave people in fear for the rest of their lives. The word NO is like a double-edged sword: on one end people will do anything to avoid hearing it, yet, on the other end people have a hard time ever saying it. As difficult as it is, the pain of rejection through the word NO is necessary.

From NOs to YES

You will never find a noteworthy successful person who has achieved anything great without going through the NOs. The NOs are essential to your growth. Howard Shultz founder of Starbucks Coffee, heard NO from 217 of the 242 investors he initially approached, before he got Starbucks going. Imagine if he had stopped trying after the 217th NO? Arianna Huffington had a book that was rejected by 36 publishers and suffered an embarrassing campaign for governor of California before she built the Huffington Post. Imagine if she had stopped after the 36th NO? Imagine if Kevin Hart, the wildly successful comedian, had quit after having chicken wings thrown at him during his first comedy show at the Laff House in Philadelphia? Imagine if he had quit after that publically embarrassing NO? Overcomers of Dreamicide who keep going after hearing NO not only have the ability to achieve their dreams, but to also sustain their dreams for the long term. The NOs are necessary. After some time, you will grow numb to the pain of rejection; you will accept it as a part of the process. If you knew that you would hear 99 NOs, but the hundredth request would result in a YES that would catapult your dreams, what would you do? You would aggressively pursue more NOs knowing that your breakthrough was coming. Well, that's exactly what happens; every NO brings you closer to the realization of your dreams. The only contention in the matter is that we can't predict exactly how many NOs we will endure before finally getting to that YES.

The Pain of Resistance

Even when doors begin to open, every Overcomer of Dreamicide will encounter resistance. Resistance is defined as the attempt to prevent something by action or argument. Every noble idea that has gone against the status quo has faced great resistance and so will your dreams. You should know that there will be people who develop the equivalent of a dissertation to go against your ideas, some might even take drastic measures to block your dreams entirely. Try not to feel offended; some of these people honestly believe they are doing it for your best interest. Resistance could come from a family member who doesn't believe you have what it takes to accomplish the goal. The rationale in this case would be to protect you from heartbreak. Others would rather see you remain where you are to avoid feeling like a failure themselves. Perhaps in other cases, you might face resistance because your plans disrupt the daily methods of operation to which people have become accustomed. Most often, resistance stems from people who fear the unknown and would rather choose the certainty of comfort over the uncertainty of change. No matter the reason, overcoming resistance will build your strength.

The Dreams of Joseph

A great story about overcoming resistance can be found in Genesis, the first book of the Bible. The Bible character known as Joseph was a young man who had many Divine dreams. His dreams indicated that he would one day rise to great prominence, and be ruler over all the land and his family. With great exuberance, Joseph shared these dreams with his family, but while he saw these dreams as Divine Blessings, his brothers and father found the dreams to be insulting. Joseph's brothers became jealous and devised a plan to kill him. Eventually, they abandoned the plan, and decided to sell him into slavery. The brothers then faked Joseph's death, which caused his father to go into a great depression. Joseph, thereafter, spent his life working as a slave under Potiphar, a man who served as captain of the guards in the king's palace. After consistently being a good and faithful servant, Joseph was eventually viewed favorably and later rose to great prominence in the land under the king. In the face of resistance, Joseph focused on executing to the highest degree, regardless of those who opposed his rise.

Joseph's story demonstrates how dreams could become reality even in the face of great resistance. The key to overcoming resistance is to remember that it's a fleeting phase. Embrace this quote from the classic movie, *Pearl Harbor*: "Victory belongs to those who believe in it the most and believe in it the longest." To overcome painful resistance, you need to exercise faithful persistence.

The Pain of Ridicule

Do you remember the childhood saying, "Sticks and stones can break my bones, but words will never hurt me"? Well, whoever created the saying was right to the extent that words can't cause physical damage. But what they should have disclosed to us was that words can cause great emotional and psychological damage. So much, that words can permanently paralyze your progress. As a matter of fact, so many dreams have met their tragic demise as a result of the pain of ridicule.

Your dreams might very well face mockery, sarcasm, and parody, and so much more as you decide to fully pursue. People will talk, laugh, and even dismiss your dreams as a practical joke. Can you imagine walking into a room where there is a committee meeting of your family members, friends, and foes discussing you and your dreams? From one end, you might hear, "There he goes again, with another business idea." On the other end you might hear, "She should just quit before getting started." The thought of this type of banter happening behind your back, or in front of your face might be enough to stop you from pursing your dreams.

You must come to grips with the reality that ridicule is painful and will surely be encountered. *Whether your dream is driven by practicality or passion, you will always find someone waiting with a dose of heart-wrenching ridicule to share with you.* No dream is immune to ridicule; however, Overcomers of Dreamicide choose to ignore it and move forward regardless of what has been said. What you must determine is whether or not the whispers of the naysayers are more important than the loud cries of your inner passion. Those who are unwilling to work hard and hustle usually prefer to sit back and "Hate." What they fail to realize is, if they would hustle as much as they hate, their lives could be different. I once saw a meme that read, "Hustle until your haters ask if you're hiring." This statement epitomizes the mindset of a person who will overcome Dreamicide. Overcomers know that people will talk, but just like lions are not concerned with the opinions of sheep, Overcomers of Dreamicide are not concerned with the opinions of people who only choose to ridicule.

Your Dream's Epidural

To reduce the pain during the birthing process of your dreams, I highly suggest undergoing the epidural procedure. The epidural may be temporarily uncomfortable and somewhat painful, but this procedure will help you get through all the previous pains mentioned. Let me tell you about the Discipline Epidural.

The Discipline Epidural

To follow a strict regimen is often very difficult. Contrary to what some personal development experts may suggest, a passion for your dreams does not automatically mean you will remain disciplined in your efforts to accomplish those dreams. Often we don't even recognize how undisciplined we are. People usually measure progress by grand gestures. They look at the big steps they made. You finally paid for the gym membership, you registered the business, or you've scheduled the audition. While those grand gestures are good first steps, the question you have to answer is, will you be disciplined enough to work out three days a week? Will you be consistent in your marketing efforts to find new customers, even when business slows down? Will you practice your routine daily before the audition? The grand gesture is just the start; the key is to repeatedly do the activities that are necessary to build momentum and achieve the desired results. Discipline isn't developed overnight. Be prepared to endure some inconsistencies in your efforts, and when you do, just remember to forgive yourself, because you're not perfect. Give yourself grace and be patient. Your dream is a journey; it will take time to get yourself together. Overcomers of Dreamicide have gone through the start-and-stop phases, and every time they start again it has made them stronger, even in moments when they felt disappointed for not following through in the first place. As long as you keep on doing what needs to be done, you will eventually achieve your desired outcome. Discipline is often a painful process, but quitting will ultimately bring you greater pain. Business philosopher Jim Rohn said it best: "We must all suffer from one of two pains: the pain of discipline or the pain of regret. The difference is that discipline weighs ounces but regret weighs tons." The choice is yours. Will you choose discipline or regret? I'm urging you to Choose Discipline!

Are Your Dreams Worth the Pain?

Now that you've read the disclaimer outlining the pains you will experience and the optional procedure for pain relief; are your dreams still worth it? Absolutely Yes! The pain endured is what makes the progress rewarding. There is no progress without pain, because the price of progress is pain. It never feels good when you're going through it, but trust me when I tell you—the scenery at the top of the mountain makes the scrapes and cuts of the grueling climb worth it. Are you willing to make the DECISION to move forward, or will you abort your dream altogether?

SUMMARY TAKEAWAYS

Progress = Pain

» The more progress you make, the more pain you will endure. Embrace pain as a part of the process. Your pain will push you to be a greater version of yourself, so that you not only attain the dream but also sustain it for the long run. Your dream is worth the pain.

$D > R^3$ (Discipline is greater than Rejection, Resistance, and Ridicule)

» Discipline will always be more powerful than the pains of Rejection, Resistance, and Ridicule. Remain consistent and remember that disciplined consistency makes a big difference.

WHAT'S NEXT?

» Developing self-discipline is essential to your growth, but it's often easy to fall back into old habits that have become second nature to you. To become more disciplined, follow this four-step process to improve your results:

1. Become clear about your desired outcome
2. Identify potential distractions
3. Remove temptations
4. Schedule your daily actions.

In the table provided, list three areas in which you would like to become more self-disciplined in pursuit of your dreams.

AREAS IN NEED OF IMPROVED SELF-DISCIPLINE	YOUR POTENTIAL DISTRACTIONS	STRATEGIES TO REMOVE TEMPTATION	SCHEDULE YOUR ACTIONS
Ex. Reduce time scrolling through posts on Facebook.	Receiving alerts on my phone about status updates.	Remove Facebook app from my phone for 3 weeks.	Periodic check-up on Facebook only at 3pm and 9pm.
1.			
2.			
3.			

DYING TO LIVE: DECISIONS DETERMINE DESTINY

The important thing is this: to be able,
at any moment, to sacrifice what we
are for what we could become.

—MAHARISHI MAHESH YOGI,
INDIAN SPIRITUAL LEADER

Whoever seeks to preserve his life will lose
it, but whoever loses his life will keep it.

LUKE 17:33 ESV

Personal development guru Les Brown stated, "If you're casual about your dream, then your dream will end up a casualty." This statement is one that I believe epitomizes the reason behind the death of so many dreams. For too long you may have treated your dreams casually. You may have made the mistake of becoming comfortable treating your dreams like an illegitimate stepchild. When one really takes full custody and responsibility for their dreams, they never neglect providing the attention, affection, and appreciation that is necessary for its healthy development. Perhaps you've become entangled in the culture of giving more of your time and attention to someone else's dreams while ultimately neglecting the dreams that belong to you. Maybe you're still more concerned about receiving approval from family, friends, and even foes that you haven't given yourself permission to follow your heart.

Does this sound like it could be you? If it does, here is what you must know: nothing happens without a made up mind. The life or death of your dreams will be determined by whether or not you decide to take full custody and responsibility for its successful outcome. Will you decide to make this a nonnegotiable priority? Will this be, for you, the equivalent to what the President of the United States would consider a matter of national security? How serious are you willing to take your dreams? Are you willing to do whatever it takes to remove the "Weapons of Mass Distraction" that often detour your focus? Until you make what author Mark Batterson calls the Defining Decision, you will never experience the Defining Moment that gives life to your dreams. Overcoming Dreamicide will not be a function of your current circumstances or conditions, but a function of your decisions. Your decisions will determine your destiny. Consequently, the decision to keep your dreams alive is also the decision to die to unsustainable thoughts, actions and habits.

The Decision to Die

As ironic as it may sound, if you really want your dreams to live, you must first decide to die. Now, I only mean this figuratively. You don't literally commit suicide to overcome Dreamicide. What I mean is this: you must be willing to die to who you are now to give birth to whom you must become to keep your dreams alive.

Here is the reality that we all must face: We are the result of our rituals. We are the result of the things we repeatedly do. As human beings, we are creatures of habit. If you were to examine your life and analyze your daily actions, what you would recognize is that you have certain patterns. Think of the approximate time that you wake up every morning. What foods do you frequently eat? What type of entertainment do you generally enjoy? If you find yourself repeatedly doing the same activities, it's because your mind, body, and soul have become accustomed to your rituals. I'm sure you can agree that what you currently have is based on what you've done thus far. Therefore, if you intend on elevating to a higher level where your dreams could live abundantly, it would require your rituals to be adjusted. You will have to let excuses die and give birth to new processes.

Let Excuses Die; Give Birth to Execution

At the crime scene of every dead dream, the easiest evidence to find is the excuse, a well-crafted justification to explain why someone failed to execute a task. Excuses are at the center in every case of Dreamicide; they serve as vindication that your failure to launch was out of your control. Excuses are like an airborne disease that we just can't avoid. We've all, at some point, been infected with a dose of what David J. Schwartz called "Excusitis"—the venomous poison that paralyzes our ability to take action because of our excuses. You know the symptoms, "I don't have enough support," "the monetary resources are not available," "the system was set up to keep me out," and "I don't have enough time." Yep, it's always the same symptoms.

Spoiler alert: it's impossible to achieve excellence with excuses. As a matter of fact, excuses only sound good to the person using them, but in the end, you know it's just an excuse. The excuses that killed your dreams were the reasons that propelled others to live and achieve theirs.

Obstacle or Opportunity? Similar Circumstances, Different Outcomes

I once heard about two brothers who grew up in an impoverished inner-city neighborhood. Both Christopher and James experienced the same circumstances in their upbringing. The boys grew up in a single-parent household, after witnessing years of their mother being a victim of domestic violence at the hands of their father. Unfortunately, their father lived a life deeply entrenched in crime, drugs, and pimping prostitutes. This eventually left them in a fatherless home. Adding insult to injury, the boys were despised by their mother because of their physical resemblance to their estranged father.

As the brothers grew older, they began taking different paths. Christopher had gone astray and started to live a life similar to his father's. Late-night partying became the norm; lots of alcohol and excessive encounters with the criminal justice system became his lifestyle. James, on the other hand, took a more righteous path. He excelled academically, was heavily involved in his community, and developed a deep interest in engineering, which later landed him a great career.

The brothers were reunited at a family gathering, and while seated at their grandmother's dinner table, the men were engaged in separate but similar conversations. They were both asked, "Why did you choose the lifestyle you currently have?" Christopher responded, "With the type of father I had, there was no choice for me but to live this hard-knock life. It was impossible for me to live any other way. If my father was present, maybe I would have turned out better, but all I've seen as my example was my father's life of crime. I'm just the product of my father's decisions."

James on the other hand, had quite a different perspective. He responded, "With the type of father I had, it was essential for me to succeed. I promised myself that I would avoid living the type of delinquent life that he lived. I was determined to be a better man, father, and role model than he ever was for my brother and me. My father being absent gave me an example of what I would never want to become; he chose a life of crime over his family, and he chose fast money over his fatherly responsibilities. I am his child, but I will never be his decisions. I've chosen a different path because of him."

Mind boggling isn't it? Did you get that? The brothers had the same circumstances, but one used the father as an excuse for his poor decisions, while the other used his father as a driving force to execute and live his dreams. Hearing this story made me ask the question: Are obstacles really obstacles, or are they disguised opportunities for growth? It's all a matter of your perspective.

Examine the excuses that you've been using to justify your inability to execute. Ask yourself, has anyone successful had the same or similar circumstances, but somehow figured out how to overcome them? The answer is ABSOLUTELY YES! Remember, everyone who came before you had less than you. People from the eighteen hundreds did not have access to the resources you have today—they created the resources. What does that tell you? If you can't find a way, then create a way.

So here is the prognosis, you can choose to cling to your excuses, which will lead to the inevitable death of your dreams, or you can commit to a full course of treatment using the antidote to counter Excusitis—*consistent execution.*

Execution Builds Momentum

If your dream has been inactive for a while, it will surely need a reboot. Often the most difficult task is to move from intention to execution. The biggest hindrance that we face is the psychological battle that we go through, believing that we must start with a bang or not start at all. The truth is, small actions make a huge difference—especially when done consistently. The decision to give birth to execution isn't easy, but it's necessary.

Grandpa Had a Stroke

At the age of seventy-four my grandfather had a stroke. The doctors informed him that although the stroke caused considerable damage, his chances for recovery were positive. He was immediately airlifted to Johns Hopkins Rehabilitation Center, where he would undergo treatment and therapy. Research indicates that it is normal for victims of a stroke to feel angry, anxious, or depressed, and so it was for my grandfather. He waited in the hospital bed hoping for a quick fix solution. The limbs on the right side of his body were weak and required consistent exercise to become strong enough to resume normal use. In the beginning, he followed the instructions of the hospital staff. The results were promising. He was able to feed himself and carry out basic hygienic functions on his own. But, unfortunately, after a few days of being frustrated with what he considered to be a slow pace of recovery, my grandfather began ignoring instructions and reduced his level of daily exercises. A few days later his condition became worse. His lack of consistent exercise led to his inability to feed and take care of himself independently. My grandfather grew more discouraged, leading him to blame the hospital staff, including his nurses and therapist for not doing enough. *What we often fail to understand is that when execution is abandoned, excuses and blame begin to creep in.* It became increasingly difficult for my grandfather to make progress, because he started to believe in his well-crafted justification as to why his conditions weren't improving.

At that moment, my mother and other family members were concerned. They attempted to convince my grandfather that he needed to take action. They began reminding him of how great he was doing and how much he could *gain*, if he followed the instructions of the staff. My perspective was a bit different; I argued that he wouldn't take action without understanding WHY he urgently needed to resume his exercise. My grandfather didn't need to hear how much he could gain—he needed to be reminded of how much he could lose. *Decisions become very urgent when we recognize that we could suffer great loss.* In the field of psychology, this is referred to as loss aversion. The basic premise of the theory suggests that *the grief of losing is stronger than the pleasure of gaining.* And guess what—it worked.

The decision to execute became much easier for him, once he understood that inaction would lead to him spending the rest of his days being handled by caretakers. A man with as much pride in his independence as my grandfather could not live with that result. When the scenario was explained, my grandfather immediately decided to resume his daily exercises, and shortly thereafter was able to feed himself again. My grandfather understood the urgent need for him to abandon his excuses and focus on execution. As it relates to decision-making, the fear of loss is often more powerful than the potential to gain. Overcomers of Dreamicide understand this principle, and it's the driving force behind their decision to make things happen.

Have you taken a moment to think of what your inability to execute means for you, your family, and your dreams? Maybe deep inside you enjoy working for that nagging boss who consistently criticizes you. Perhaps you're prepared to spend the next ten, or probably twenty, years residing in the same neighborhood. Maybe you don't really mind that terrible feeling that you experience every time you're unable to financially assist your loved ones when they're in a difficult situation.

Maybe it's not that big of a deal that you can't visit those countries that you've always dreamed about. When you refuse to make the decision to execute, you decide to sustain your current conditions.

We all have great intentions, but well intended does not mean well executed. We can't pay bills, accomplish goals, or keep our dreams alive with intentions; it will only happen with consistent action. Until you let all your excuses pass away, you will never give birth to execution.

Let Negative History Die, Give Birth to New Destiny

Imagine dating someone who does nothing besides complain about their past relationship? All they speak about is the wrong that was previously done to them and how much they hate that they tolerated it for so long. Imagine you plan a trip for the both of you, only to spend the entire trip discussing all that went wrong in their previous trips with their ex-lover? The discussion would undeniably create an uncomfortable atmosphere, and may immediately cause you to end the relationship. It's difficult to drive forward, looking backward. As the driver of your dreams, you need to spend more time looking through the windshield as opposed to the rearview mirrors. If not, tragic accidents are certain to happen. It's unsafe for you to drive your dreams forward while looking backward. You will always experience misery if your thoughts are constantly consumed with the mishaps of your history. *Your past should only serve as a point of reference, not your permanent residence.*

The Lifeline

Your past is your past and, to be candid, you can't do anything about it. The only productive path moving forward would be to make the most of your present moment in the hopes of securing a better future. To illustrate this point, allow me to share with you what I call the Lifeline. Let's imagine that your life was depicted in a single line. You would draw a horizontal line from left to right on a piece of paper; this would represent your lifeline. At the left is the beginning of your life starting at zero. To the far right end of the horizontal line is your life expectancy. Let's say, for example, the average person may live to be eighty-five years old. Now, in the middle of your lifeline, I want you to place your current age; for purposes of the illustration, let's use thirty-three. Now that your lifeline is created, I want you to subtract your current age from your expected life expectancy. For example, I would subtract thirty-three from eighty-five, which would give me fifty-two. Everything to the right of your current age is how many years you have left to live. Everything to the left of your age is what has already passed. There is absolutely nothing you can do about your past; the only thing you can control is what you do now, which will shape what happens in your future. It baffles me when people spend so much time talking about their history. What they used to do, how they used to be, what people used to say about them. To be quite honest, you could continue to reminisce about your past, but people are more interested in who you are now. It's imperative that you let go of your history and start to focus on your destiny. If I have fifty-two more years ahead of me, that means fifty-two more years of opportunities for potential growth, progress, family gatherings, and many more memorable moments. This should serve as a reminder that there is more to look forward to than there is in your past. See the sample illustration on the following page.

THE LIFELINE

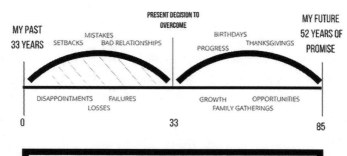

DECISIONS DETERMINE DESTINY

Let Old Habits Die, Give Birth to New Traits

To keep your dreams alive, there are a number of counter-productive habits that you will have to give up entirely. To identify what those habits are requires a high level of honesty, unfiltered truthfulness, and self-awareness. You can't be who you want to become and who you were at the same time. Everyone has to give up to go up. Stop trying to bring old habits into your new dimension.

I Gave Up Partying

My mother could tell you, when I was younger, my home was where I slept but not where I lived. So much of my time was spent roaming the streets and partying. I always wanted to be on the road. I rarely found time to be in the house. My routine was school, work, party, sleep, then repeat. Week after week, I would engage is this behavior. I never got enough rest, until I started recognizing that this was unsustainable. I was spending money; I had no savings and nothing to show for my life. I worked as a pizza chef during the week and washed cars at a jeep rental company during the weekends. I was very active but not productive. It wasn't until I moved to New York that this lifestyle started to shift. If I was going to grow into a new me, I needed to shift and get rid of some of my old habits. Partying was one of those activities that I gave up. But giving up habits isn't enough; you have to replace those old habits with new ones.

I believe our old habits leave clues that can be used for positive new traits. For example, my school, work, party, sleep, and repeat cycle became very useful for me when I had to balance school, work, family, and business. You see, my partying activity was replaced with family time. My ability to be consistent and handle multiple projects simultaneously became a strength for me over the years and allowed me to become a more well-rounded individual. I'm not perfect, but I'm still making progress, and the urge to party all the time is no longer a habit of mine. But the ability to keep a consistent cycle of activities has been beneficial.

Examine Your Habits

What are some of the habits that you must abandon to propel yourself to the next dimension? If you have a hard time figuring it out on your own, I would suggest you create a safe space for the people who are closest to you to gather. When they are all together, give them the opportunity to provide you with unfiltered feedback about what they find to be some of your weaknesses or counterproductive habits. Take the information and immediately work on identifying how you could begin shifting those old habits and developing new traits. I promise you, letting counterproductive habits die will give birth to a better and stronger you.

SUMMARY TAKEAWAYS

We must die to live

» For your dreams to live, you have to let habits die that are not aligned with your desired destiny. You can't be who you were and who you want to become at the same time.

Self-assess or self-destruct

» It's imperative that you examine your daily habits, discussions, and behavior. One of the most detrimental actions you can take is to not be self-aware. Without knowing yourself, your dream is destined to meet its demise.

WHAT'S NEXT?

» Knowing the costs of indecision helps to place everything into perspective. In the illustration below, create a short list describing what ignoring your dream will cost you versus how pursuing your dream will benefit you. Whenever you feel like giving up or postponing your dream, go back to this illustration to be reminded of what's on the line.

WEIGHING THE COSTS VS. BENEFITS OF YOUR DECISIONS

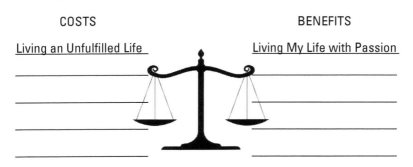

COSTS	BENEFITS
Living an Unfulfilled Life	Living My Life with Passion

SECTION II

meth·od
meTHəd/

noun
plural noun: **methods**

A particular form of procedure for
accomplishing or approaching something,
especially a systematic or established one.

THE OVERCOMERS' METHODS

*Someone else has already achieved the level of success
you desire. Reinventing the wheel is therefore an act of
unproductive exploration. Your dream has a manual
that is currently in use by someone else; it would be of
great value for you to find that manual and begin
using it as a starting point.*

*Overcomers are confident that discovering,
developing, and deploying the strategies that were
proven effective for others will increase the likelihood
of achieving the same results, if followed. Copy and
paste may not be acceptable in school, but it's allowed
in life. It's not a problem to follow the methods of
high-performing achievers.*

SYSTEMS FOR SUCCESS: FOLLOW THE DREAMPRINTS

> Success leaves clues. Go figure out what someone
> who was successful did, and model it. Improve
> it, but learn their steps. They have knowledge.
> —Tony Robbins

> What has been will be again, what has
> been done will be done again; there
> is nothing new under the sun.
> Ecclesiastes 1:9 niv

I'm often perplexed when I hear self-help authors, motivational speakers, and personal development experts discuss the topic of achieving success. It seems as if almost every book written, speech delivered, or conference attended begins with the same claim. "Today, you will learn *the Secret*." What usually proceeds is a litany of characteristics that one must exhibit to achieve success. You know the usual suspects: characteristics like desire, work ethic, positive attitude, persistence, passion, enthusiasm, commitment . . . The list goes on and on. Although I wholeheartedly agree that all of these suggestions are true, my only contention is the claim that this happens to be "a secret." It's so ironic, because by sheer definition, a secret shouldn't be known by the masses. If these secrets were supposed to be hidden, it would appear to be a poorly kept secret to begin with. Rarely do we hear anything that hasn't been said before.

Please forgive me; earlier in my speaking career, I used to make the same bold claim that I also had "the Secret to Success." It was only as I evolved and matured that I came to the realization that as it relates to success and achieving your dreams, there really are no secrets—only Systems.

A World of Systems

Our entire world is operated by Systems. To define System, I like the definition provided by BusinessDictionary.com: *A set of detailed methods, procedures and routines created to carry out a specific activity, perform a duty, or solve a problem.*

Systems are reliable, because their processes have already been proven to be effective and/or efficient. When a System is followed correctly, specific outcomes are predictable. Today, many of the largest companies in the world are the result of great Systems that were created, replicated, and repeated in different geographic locations. McDonald's has a great System for the delivery of fast food. Walmart has a great System to provide goods at a low cost. FedEx has a great System for the expeditious delivery of packages. Amazon has a great System for providing inexpensive products, with fast shipping and reliable online service. The common denominator among these thriving organizations is this: they've all developed great Systems. The reason these companies continue to thrive has nothing to do with their Secrets. Everything has a System, and as it relates to your dreams, there is a System for Success.

Systems for Success

Mr. Hamou, a well-established entrepreneur, met my wife Shereece at her job in August 2013. Shereece was a registered nurse at the time and was taking care of his mother, who had suffered a broken hip. Delighted with the service of care his mother received, he sparked a discussion and began asking my wife questions about her professional aspirations and her family life. Shereece began to tell him about her short-term goals of becoming a nurse practitioner. She also informed him that I was a professor, political consultant, and personal empowerment speaker. Intrigued by the conversation, he proceeded to independently research my background online. He came across some of my weekly YouTube videos and decided to reach out. Mr. Hamou expressed that he was impressed by my work and proposed a business opportunity for us to potentially collaborate. At the time, I was working on a major business proposal, teaching nine courses at the college, participating in several ministries at my church, and consulting on a heavily contested political campaign; all of this while simultaneously taking on speaking engagements. If you searched for the definition of "busy" at the time, you would probably see my picture on the side. I expressed to Mr. Hamou that while I was flattered by the offer, I just had too much on my plate. He puzzled me immediately thereafter by asking where did I want to be in ten years. Clueless as to why he asked, I respectfully requested that he clarify the purpose for his questioning. He responded, "If you want to know where you will be ten years from now, look at someone who has been doing the same thing ten years longer than you. If you follow the same path, that's where you will be." I immediately thought about everyone I knew who complained about being extremely busy, but were busy being broke, busted, and disgusted. If I continued following the systems of unfocused busyness that got them to where they were, I would end up being in relatively the same place.

Mr. Hamou suggested that I never ignore an opportunity because I'm busy, but determine whether the opportunity was aligned with the long-term vision of where I desired to be personally or professionally. He said, "There is someone already doing what you hope to accomplish; follow their steps and you will get those results, but you must become less busy and more focused." His business proposition would have given me access to people who had already accomplished my aspirations on a grand scale in the public speaking industry. Through this opportunity, I would have been exposed to people such as John C. Maxwell, Tony Robbins, Les Brown, and many more. Mr. Hamou ended our conversation by saying, "The most expensive thing one can have is a closed mind, because closed minds usually close doors and cost us big opportunities." I took heed of those words and started investigating the Systems that were followed, and in some cases created, by the authors and speakers that I admired.

The experience with Mr. Hamou taught me an important principle: if both success and failure leave footprints, then accomplished dreams must leave dreamprints. Overcomers of Dreamicide know that if you want to expedite the process toward the realization of your dreams, you must find, study, follow, then disrupt the Systems that have been left by others. With that being said, it's time to get practical!

Finding the System

The Internet, without a doubt, has transformed our ability to find information. Information has never been more accessible than it is today—it only makes sense that we take advantage of these technological advancements. Your current dreams are being accomplished somewhere, somehow, by someone. And if these people are consistently achieving great results, it's not because they're lucky; it's because they've found a strategy or System. I view the acronym S.Y.S.T.E.M. as a methodology to **S**ave **Y**our **S**elf **T**ime **E**nergy and **M**oney. A good System will help you to avoid the pitfalls and mistakes experienced by others. A good System will improve your effectiveness and efficiency as you pursue excellent results. By now, I hope you get my point. Find a good System.

Practical Steps to Find Your System

Make a list of between five to ten people that are living the life that you desire or accomplishing the goals that you are dreaming about. Are any of them sharing their stories? Do they have books or biographies about their respective journeys? Do they have a website, video channel, podcast, or courses offering this information? Have they done interviews discussing their accomplishments? Are you following them via social media? If you haven't found this information yet, search for it immediately. It's imperative that you become a student of the person's work. Whether or not you have the resources to easily access this information, I would suggest that you research their contact information and send an e-mail, write a letter, or make a phone call to introduce yourself. Whatever methodology you choose, explain how and why you admire their work, and ask for an opportunity to do an interview. It may seem like a long shot, but guess what, you will miss 100 percent of the shots you don't take. Create between five to seven questions that are pertinent to understanding their journey and document the conversation if access is granted. On the following page you will find sample language to use for your correspondence.

Good Morning <u>Name of Person</u>,

My name is <u>YOUR NAME</u>, and over the years I've greatly admired the work that you do as a <u>area of expertise</u>. Your work has truly reinvigorated what it means to be a <u>title for people from that industry</u> in the 21st century, and I am eternally grateful for your contribution. As an aspiring <u>area of expertise</u> myself, I would love the opportunity to learn more about the life experiences that have shaped your thinking to have such a profound worldview. At your convenience, I am respectfully requesting an opportunity for a <u>fifteen-minute</u> phone conference or face-to-face introductory meeting.

Who Should You Target?

My suggestion would be to identify individuals on three different levels: those who have just started (1–3 years), those who are more seasoned in the journey (5–9 years), and those who are veterans in the game (10 or more years). As you go through this process, be sure to diversify your subjects. While it's easy to find information on celebrities, world-class performers, and/or pioneers of an industry, you should also search for information on lesser-known individuals who are maintaining or thriving in your area of interest. It might be the local artist who is well known in your neighborhood; maybe you'll talk to a business owner who has operated his or her business for over ten years. The System works anywhere, no matter how much notability someone has or doesn't have. As a matter of fact, the people who are local will, more than likely, be easier to access than those with more fame and prestige. After you've found the System, it's time to study and dissect it.

Study the System

Whether or not you enjoyed school, studying was always highly recommended as a task to complete if you wanted to do well academically. Studying should have been added to your daily chores. When studying the System of your dreams, I've discovered that it's an enjoyable task that arouses great excitement. As you're studying these Systems, I want you to become a "Pattern Recognition Expert." Look for patterns in approaches, required work ethic, and social surroundings. You will find that successful Systems have patterns that are easily recognizable.

Every instruction manual, at a minimum, informs you about best practices (Tips), needed materials (Tools), and the processes for assembly (Techniques). As you are finding the information about the Systems used by these achievers, you should take notes in that order. Your sole purpose is to create a chart mapping out the Tips, Tools, and Techniques deployed by those who are living your dreams. Take note of the routines, books, common practices, or questions they've utilized to guide their decision making and implementation processes.

Once you've completed your analysis, it's time to apply what you've discovered. The knowledge is good, but it must be implemented. Ignorance on fire is far better than knowledge on ice. Knowing everything but not applying it is the equivalent of not knowing anything at all.

Follow the System

Earlier in this chapter, I mentioned a few examples of organizations that created and operated effective systems. Among those organizations was the McDonald's Corporation. The reason I highlight McDonald's is because they are what I consider to be the epitome of "Systems Thinking."

The company's founder, Ray Kroc, wanted to build a restaurant system that would be famous for providing food of consistently high quality and uniform methods of preparation. "Systems First" was his guiding philosophy. This meant that every single ingredient was tested, tasted, and perfected to fit the operating system. In 1961, Kroc launched a training program, later known as Hamburger University. At Hamburger University, franchisees were trained on the proper methods for running a successful McDonald's restaurant. If you ever intended on opening a McDonald's franchise, you would be required to adhere to the systems approach and methods taught at Hamburger University. While many of McDonald's most famous menu items like the Big Mac, Filet-O-Fish, and Egg McMuffin were created by franchisees, the McDonald's operating system required franchisees to follow the core McDonald's principles. In other words, I couldn't open a McDonald's and then decide to design the interior like Red Lobster. McDonald's requires you to FOLLOW THEIR SYSTEM.

So how does this McDonald's illustration relate to your dreams? Well, if you want to be successful in a certain arena, you should at least understand the prerequisites of that industry. For example, if you're thinking of running an online business, a prerequisite is to ensure that your website is gaining traffic, leads, and conversions. Without it, you're not even in the game. Every system has prerequisites and tenets that are the foundation of keeping it together. Sports require consistent workout routines, entrepreneurship requires risk taking, the field of sales requires prospecting. Once you find the prerequisites of your system, you need to be coachable to following the system and getting the basics in place. Now, don't get me wrong, you may not have to operate on the same level as the top performers of the industry. It's important that you start where you are with what you have. Many of the top performers that we see today have been working on their craft for decades. We see the glory but often don't know the story behind their success. That's why you just need to make sure you're following the basic prerequisites of the system. After achieving the basics, the last step sounds a bit radical, but it's necessary. It's time to "Disrupt the System"

Disrupt the System

The previous section about Following the System, may have you questioning whether I'm merely suggesting that you copy your way to the attainment of your dreams. Absolutely not. I believe that you were born original, so there is no need to live entirely like a copy. If you want to break out of the traditional, your next step would be to disrupt the system. One of the most followed podcasters is Tim Ferriss, and I love what he wrote in his book, *Tools of Titans*. He wrote, "Borrow liberally, combine uniquely, and create your own bespoke blueprint." In essence, if you want to be a game changer in a room full of players, you need to use your unique approach to innovate the system. This is what disruption is all about. Finding the gaps in the system and filling them with something that adds tremendous value. I would suggest that you search for gaps in at least one of five primary categories. These may be gaps in information, leadership, resources, technology, or solutions. When you successfully fill these gaps, your approach becomes the new standard for which others will strive to meet.

Modern Day Disruptors

Over the last decade we've seen major shifts in various industries due to increased use of the Internet, smartphones, apps software, and social media. Services and products have been highly customized, convenient, and connected to communities. To substantiate this point, look at the illustration on the following page.

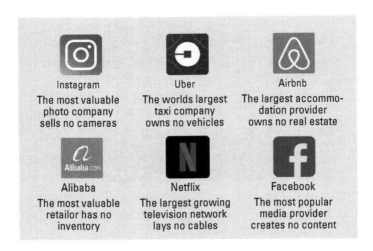

How astonishing is that? When I first saw this image online, it was an eye opener for me. This is a clear depiction of what modern day disruption looks like.

The Uber Disruption

According to Uber.com, on a snowy Paris evening in 2008, Travis Kalanick and Garrett Camp had trouble hailing a cab. So they came up with a simple idea—tap a button and get a ride. What started as an app to request premium black cars in a few metropolitan areas is now changing the logistical fabric of cities around the world. Whether it's a ride, a sandwich, or a package, Uber uses technology to satisfy consumers' needs and wants at their convenience.

Taxicabs were an invention of the seventeenth century, and as time went by, individuals continued to innovate the system. We went from horse-drawn carriages, originally known as Hackney carriages, to hansom cabs, to electric battery–powered taxis, to automobiles. With all of this history, how in the world did Uber become a major player in the transportation industry of today? Ponder this: the way Uber disrupted the taxi and limousine industry was not with a more innovative mode of transportation, but with an APP that provided users quick and convenient access to transportation via a mobile device. A software company disrupted the taxi industry. Game changer!

Ready to Disrupt?

Before you can disrupt a System, you must first understand how the System works. You have to understand the industry and your area of expertise. You have to know the pulse of the consumers. You have to identify where these consumers need more value and determine how you can supply it. This is not a one-time process, and it doesn't matter where you are as it relates to your dreams. Overcomers of Dreamicide continually engage in this process to keep up to date and remain relevant. Once you have this foundation in place, the next step would be to gain absolute clarity about the mark you hope to leave on the System.

SUMMARY TAKEAWAYS

Stop looking for Secrets; search for Systems

» Don't get caught in the trap of believing that there are Secrets to success. The Systems that exist are being replicated and expanded every day. Someone has achieved the level that you are aspiring to reach. Research their steps and follow their systems to success.

Ask and it might be given

» Never hesitate to reach out to those individuals who are already making progress. You have nothing to lose but potentially a whole lot to gain. Plant your outreach seeds, and soon it will land on fertile soil.

Fill the gaps

» To be a game changer, your focus needs to be on filling the gaps. The gaps that exist in various industries give you room to innovate by providing solutions to those issues. Entrepreneurs are people who generate profits by solving problems.

WHAT'S NEXT?

» Create a chart to document the tips, tools, and techniques provided by the achievers, world-class performers, and icons that you admire.

ADMIRED ACHIEVER	TIPS (BEST PRACTICES)	TOOLS	TECHNIQUES (HOW TO STEPS)
Ex. Name of world-class performer	• Routines • Common Practices	• Books • Apps • Events	• Approach • Perspective • Daily habits
1.			
2.			
3.			

» » » 6 « « «

CLARITY IS ESSENTIAL: PICTURE IT. PLAN IT. PURSUE IT.

Without vision, even the most focused
passion is a battery without a device.
—KEN AULETTA, *New Yorker* COLUMNIST

And the Lord answered me, and said,
Write the vision, and make it plain upon
tables, that he may run that readeth it.
HABAKKUK 2:2 KJV

Recently, I observed my daughter staring out the window as the train passed near my mother-in-law's house. Every time we make the trip, she sits by the window and yells the same refrain, "Look, Daddy—look at the train!" It never fails; her level of excitement is extremely high, as if it were her first time seeing a train. I thought to myself, it's amazing how toddlers see inventions like trains, airplanes, boats, and cars, and automatically have their spark reignited just from the mere sight of the invention. As they get older, they even begin to argue with their siblings, friends, or classmates about who owns what. You know what I'm talking about—"that's my car," "that's my doll," "that's my house." Although they don't own this object of their affection, one thing is for sure: they're absolutely CLEAR about what they desire, even if they're unclear about what it takes to really own and maintain it. Children show us every day what it means to have absolute clarity.

Clarity of Purpose

Bar none, gaining clarity is essential to achieving anything significant in business or life endeavors. Without clarity, one is left to be a wanderer making daily decisions without a destination in mind. Dreams die when the occupant of the dream lacks a clear picture and plan of how to grab hold of what they desire. While the thought of the dream is exciting, they later learn that what it takes to accomplish the dream is more than expected. Here's the punch line: the dream is free, but the hustle is sold separately. I believe this best sums up my point. It's easy to talk about what you want, but are you clear about why you want it and what it takes to earn it? When you gain clarity about your why and what (the Picture), you will figure out the where and when (the Plan). This will help to determine your how (the Pursuit). This process will give you absolute clarity about your dreams. The more clarity you possess, the more action you will take. If you remain unclear, you will lose enthusiasm. Over time, the thought of your dreams will become less impressive. Eventually, the chances of realizing your dreams will become a historical footnote of what you once intended to achieve.

So, how do you gain clarity? The next few pages will serve as your guide to effectively Picture, Plan, and Pursue your dreams.

Picture It

Helen Keller, the American author, political activist, and lecturer was the first deaf-blind person to earn a bachelor of arts degree. During an interview, she was asked, "What could be worse than being born blind?" In her response, she said, "The only thing worse than being blind is having sight and no vision." I thought to myself, wow—such a profound statement. Do you have sight without vision? Are you so consumed by your daily tasks that you haven't taken a moment to clearly define the big picture? Here is what I can tell you: the eyes are useless when the mind is blind. Although your eyes give you the ability to see, it is your mind that gives you the ability to imagine and create your future. Through focused thought, you have the ability to create a compelling vision that is beyond the sight of what is directly in front of you. Before your dreams can become real, they must first be envisioned in the mind. Vision gives you the mental recognition of the possibilities.

What's Your Vision?

A Biblical proverb states, "Where there is no vision, the people will perish." (Prov. 29:18 KJV) I believe this is true as it pertains to your dreams. Without a clear vision, your goals, plans and dreams will perish. So, what is your vision? How do you see yourself five, ten, or fifteen years from now? Who would you like to become? If you find yourself unsure about how to answer these questions, consider this statement by renowned technology forecaster, Daniel Burrus, "How you view the future shapes how you act in the present; how you act in the present shapes your future. Your futureview determines the future you." To gain clarity about your futureview, you need to examine your present priorities. The exercise below may be helpful.

Take a look at the illustration on the next page. On the left of this illustration is what I call the F⁷—Seven Foundational Pillars of your existence. These are the areas that set the foundation for why we do everything. On the right, you will find space to assign your Foundational priorities—the level of importance you assign to each category. Take a moment and prioritize the list from most important being 1 to least important being 7.

CATEGORY	PRIORITY #
Faith (Spiritual)	_____
Family (Familial)	_____
Friends (Relationships)	_____
Fitness (Health)	_____
Finances (Money & Wealth)	_____
Fun (Entertainment)	_____
Fulfillment (Vocation)	_____

Now that you've completed your prioritization, I want you to create a vision statement based on these priorities. Take a look at how I've prioritized mine and then create your own statement using this example as a framework.

CATEGORY	PRIORITY #
Faith	1
Family	2
Friends	5
Fitness	6
Finances	7
Fun	4
Fulfillment	3

VISION STATEMENT

Sherman Browne is a God-fearing (1) family man (2) dedicated to teaching, inspiring, encouraging, and empowering (3 & 4) my friends and all who I encounter (5) to unlock their potential, while living a healthy life & leaving a lasting legacy personally, professionally, socially and financially (6 & 7).

YOUR VISION STATEMENT

_____

_____

_____

_____

_____

_____

Have you completed your vision statement? Keep in mind, your vision statement doesn't have to be perfect; it's intended to provide direction. As you age, your priorities might change, but the core values will remain constant. Personally, I have found this exercise to be instrumental in shaping how I make decisions. Whenever I get discouraged about my dreams, I take a look at my vision statement to refocus my attention. Your vision statement is what I describe as your Life Statement. If we had to attend your funeral tomorrow, but didn't have access to your obituary or were unable to hear someone share the eulogy, your life statement should be sufficient to speak of who you were in this life.

Now that you have a clear vision statement, you need to determine, what does living your dreams look like? Here is where you need to get a blank canvas and begin to literally paint the picture of what you envision for yourself. Maybe you've heard of the concept of creating a vision board. If you haven't, a vision board is a simple yet powerful visualization tool that is often recommended to begin manifesting your dreams into reality. A vision board is simply a visual representation or collage of the things that you want to have, be, or do in your life. Many of the world's greatest achievers have cited the practice of creating a vision board as pertinent to their achievement. I've provided an example of what a vision board might look like in the figure below. The idea is to create it and place it in areas where it is visible to you (i.e. your bedroom, refrigerator, bathroom, etc.). However, I would like to take it a step further. I would suggest that you also master the practice of Self Authoring.

Vision Board Example

The Art of Self Authoring

Over the years that I've consulted organizations, one of the common habits that I've embraced is to write down the ideal outcome prior to the pursuit of my goal. There were moments when I honestly thought I developed a new idea, only to realize that I'd previously documented the thought somewhere in a notebook or on my computer. Jordan Peterson, a professor at the University of Toronto, defines this practice as Self Authoring. According to Professor Peterson, recent investigations have shown that the explicit written description of an ideal future produces similar results. A large body of research conducted in the industrial and business arenas demonstrate that the act of Self Authoring improves productivity and performance.

Self Authoring $10 Million Dollars

I'll never forget listening to the story of Canadian actor and comedian Jim Carrey. In an interview on the *Oprah Winfrey Show*, he shared the story of how in 1990 as a struggling comedian in Los Angeles, he drove to the top of a hill and made himself a millionaire. How did he do it? While sitting in his car that night, he wrote himself a check for $10 million dollars and placed in the notation line, "for acting services rendered." He dated it for Thanksgiving 1995. Carrey placed the check in his wallet. As the years progressed, the check continued to deteriorate, but by 1995 he had experienced tremendous success and learned that in that year he was going to earn $10 million dollars for his role in the hit movie, *Dumb and Dumber*. What I found fascinating was "$10 million" by 1995. While some might consider this pure coincidence, I would argue it was the result of Self Authoring. Now let me be clear, the point in sharing this story is not to say that if you just write something down it will happen.

But I am saying with absolute confidence that Self Authoring coupled with consistent effort will highly increase your chances of achieving your desired outcome.

Self Authoring Your Dreams

What will Self Authoring look like for you? The more specific you are, the better the chances you have of achieving the results. One of the biggest mistakes you can make is to generalize your dreams. When engaged in Self Authoring you need to be specific. Here are a few examples below of General Dreams versus Self Authored Dreams.

GENERAL DREAMS	SELF AUTHORED DREAMS
Start a business	Within a year, I am going to establish my portfolio and begin selling my artwork on Etsy, ebay, and other online retail outlets, which will allow me to turn my lifelong passion into profits.
Write a book	In order to establish myself as an expert, I will write a 100+ page book on engaging, educating, and empowering young women by writing one chapter per month (3–5 pages per week). The book will be completed in ten months and land me an interview on a local access television network.
Find my first client	To acquire new clients for my consulting business within two months, I will ask for referrals, launch a social media marketing campaign, and attend three networking events where prospects for my business gather.

The Implications of Self Authoring

Whether you recognize it or not, what you hope to achieve has bigger implications beyond the mere attainment of the goal. On the surface you may know that you want to make more money, but there is a deeper reason for that. Maybe it's because you want to donate more to charity, or probably you're eager to take more vacations without feeling financially challenged. You may know that you wish to work from home, but there is a deeper reason. Perhaps you have a son or daughter that you desire to spend more time with, which has made flexibility on the job more important to you. Clearly outlining the specifics will paint the picture of the WHY and WHAT you desire to accomplish. With this information you are now prepared to determine the WHEN and WHERE to implement the Plan.

Plan It

Say this with me: Proper Planning and Preparation Prevents Poor Performance. Yeah, I know—it's a mouthful. But pay attention to the principle. Your dreams won't amount to anything if there is no clear plan on how to execute. Planning your process and preparing for possible obstacles is essential to ensuring your success. If you look at the Self-Authored dreams that were created on the previous page, you will recognize that there are smaller objectives that must be met to accomplish the overall goal. If you wanted to open a business, investors and banks require more than just your ideas; they want to see a business plan. People with ideas come a dime a dozen; people who effectively Plan and execute their ideas are rare. Your plan will evolve overtime, but without a Plan your dreams will dissolve immediately.

Planning Essentials

Any Plans you create to achieve your dreams will require that you specify how you will simultaneously manage, maintain, measure, and leverage the following elements: Time, Technology, Resources, Results, and Yourself. Let's discuss these individually.

Managing and Maintaining Yourself
(It Begins and Ends with You)

You are the driving force in moving your dreams forward. Without you, your dreams don't exist. Because of this fact, a clear plan must be established for developing yourself personally, professionally, socially, and in some cases academically. You don't have a monopoly on knowledge, skills, or abilities—you have to develop a plan for your constant growth and improvement. How are you going to improve your Leadership, Teamwork, and Communication skills to make you the best person for carrying out this task? Take a moment and make a list of at least three courses, workshops, webinars, or conferences you may need to attend over the next year to stay relevant. The biggest room in the world is the room for improvement. Overcomers of Dreamicide are always improving themselves.

Managing Time

We all have twenty-four hours in a day, so why do some people complete more tasks than others? Because some people just manage their time better. Most people are not working full time on their dreams. That is not a problem, but if you want to see progress for your dreams, you will need to carve out mandatory times to work on what you desire. Rory Vaden the author of the book, *Procrastinate on Purpose: 5 Permissions to Multiply Your*

Time, uses a great tool called the Focus Funnel. You should check out his TED talk. If you search Google, you should be able to find it online.

In essence, the Focus Funnel puts the onus on you to look at all the tasks required to accomplish your goal, then forces you to ask yourself which tasks could you eliminate, automate, or delegate. This, of course, is assuming the tasks in question could be done by someone else or through technology. If the task cannot be eliminated, automated, or delegated, you must ask yourself, can it wait until later? If it can wait, then it just may be a task that could be deferred to a later date. But if not, then it's clear that you must concentrate on that task. But wait—is Rory Vaden saying that it's okay to procrastinate? Check out the excerpt below; I think it's the best explanation of this concept by Rory Vaden.

> *There's a big difference in waiting to do something you know should be done, but don't feel like doing, and waiting to do something because now is not the optimal time. Waiting because you don't feel like it is classic procrastination, and it's a cause of a mediocre life. Waiting because you're deciding to procrastinate on purpose can be considered a synonym for patience.*

So here is your homework, take some time to clearly document all the tasks that must be completed to carry out your objectives, and then put them through the Focus Funnel to help you multiply your time.

Leveraging Technology

The rise of apps, social media, and other technologies has greatly enhanced our ability to live our dreams. Technology has allowed for more efficiency and, in some cases, more effectiveness.

While some make arguments that technology has handicapped our society, I am of the thought that technology is just a tool, we have the ability to decide how we use it. Can the attainment of your dreams be expedited through technology? I would argue yes. For people who want to start businesses, the ability to market products has dramatically improved. Social media has certainly increased my presence as an expert in the field of personal development. What technologies are currently being used by people who are living your dreams, and are you leveraging the benefits of those technologies? Find a way to use what is available.

Leveraging Resources

Resource planning is essential. You have to outline the type of raw materials needed, as well as how you can attain both financial and human resources. We often spend much of our time focusing on what we don't have, as opposed to maximizing what we do have. Develop the habit of starting where you are, with what you have. As you grow, the resources will become available, but you have to start.

I must emphasize that your most important resource to get your dreams going will be your Human Resources. Your dreams need a team. People make things happen, and if you want to effectively grow and expand, you will need more than yourself. If you want to go fast, go alone, but if you want to go far—go with people. I've dedicated Chapter 8 to building your Dream Team.

Measurable Results

For every goal you're working towards, you need to have measures to track your progress. It's not enough to say you're going to lose weight without specifying how many pounds you want to lose. Your measured results should be both short term and long term. When planning, you will need to set benchmarks that you desire to reach in a required time. Make sure your measures aren't based on what others believe you should be doing. Create your own measures. When Michael Jordan was asked what made him so great at basketball, he responded, "I'm not competing with somebody else; I'm competing with what I'm capable of."

Periodic Planning Updates

As stated earlier, your plans will evolve over time, especially as circumstances begin to change in your life. Planning is a never-ending process. Designating time for yearly planning is essential. Every year, I organize a planning retreat to give me the opportunity to reflect on where I am, celebrate my progress, and prepare for my future. I would suggest that you incorporate a yearly retreat as well. Now that you have the Picture and the Plan, it's time to Pursue!

Pursue It

This section is PLAIN AND SIMPLE. GO GET IT DONE! JUST DO IT! You have the gift, the vision, and the plan. You could always seek more information, but information without application is only fascination. You have to start where you are with what you have. In the words of the great Dr. Martin Luther King Jr., "If you can't fly then run. If you can't run then walk. If you can't walk then crawl, but whatever you do, you have to keep moving forward." Please, do me this favor: be YOU and PURSUE!

SUMMARY TAKEAWAYS

Clarity gives you a clear path

» Confusion breeds frustration and stagnation. When you are unclear about what you are trying to achieve, you are easily distracted and thrown off course. Follow the exercises provided to give you absolute clarity on your path moving forward.

Leverage your resources

» Your success is not dependent on how many resources you have, but how resourceful you are. Most people grossly overestimate what they would do with what they don't have, while underestimating what they can do with what they do have. Be more resourceful in your plans and pursuits.

WHAT'S NEXT?

» Set your dates for periodic planning updates.
» Take a general dream or goal that you've created; now turn it into a self-authored dream like the illustration on page 83.

MONTHLY UPDATES	
January:	July:
Febuary:	August:
March:	September:
April:	October:
May:	November:
June:	December:

GENERAL DREAMS	SELF-AUTHORED DREAMS

» » » 7 « « «

ROAD BLOCKS: ATTACK OF THE SETBACKS (S.O.S.)

Even the accomplished suffers setbacks
sometimes. The more bitter the lessons,
the greater the successes will be.

—Lucio Tan

For I consider that the sufferings of this
present time are not worth comparing with
the glory that is to be revealed to us.

Romans 8:18 esv

The journey to your dreams will not be smooth; no matter how much you plan, you will inevitably encounter heavy traffic, major delays, detours, and roadblocks. At times, these conditions may cause you to question whether or not your dream's destination is worth the trip. Situations like personal or family tragedy, betrayals, loss of a job, or unanticipated departures by business partners will often weigh heavily on whether or not you will commit Dreamicide. Very few have the ability to turn these seemingly insurmountable obstacles into transformational opportunities for growth. To be prepared for these potential setbacks, it will serve you well to hope for the best but prepare for the worst. In other words, you'll be in a much better position if you always expect the unexpected. This is how you will prepare for the attack of the setbacks.

Unexpected Losses

In 2008, at the tender age of twenty-four, I decided to run for membership in the New York State Assembly—the lower house of the New York State Legislature. As a rising political operative who worked on various political campaigns in New York City, I had developed a great reputation for helping to win elections. After helping countless candidates win campaigns for public office, I developed an eager determination to be an elected official myself. So after just two years of residing in the Eighty-Third Assembly District of the Bronx, I decided it was my turn to win. This is what led to the launch of my campaign for public office. The incumbent at the time had been in office for eight years and had earned a well-established reputation for doing good work in the community. My blind ambition convinced me that I could make history by defying the predictions of the political pundits— although I knew the odds were against me. After months of knocking on doors, speaking at campaign rallies, and shamelessly raising money, election night had finally come. I was confident that my small team of volunteers and I had done all we could do, but I was unsure what the results would be. In New York City, local political campaigns favor the incumbent 95 percent of the time, but recognizing the wave of newly registered young voters from Barack Obama's presidential campaign, I figured we'd have a better chance of winning. I remember sitting with my wife Shereece as we awaited the results. Boy, was I surprised! After all the returns came in, I learned that I had only received 25 percent of the vote. This was a stunning blow to my ego. Embarrassed can't even begin to express the emotions I felt. Here it was, I took a leave of absence from my job to chase this dream, and I totally blew it. Not only that—I hadn't thought about what I would do if I lost the election.

To make matters worse, a year later, after returning to my job, my boss—who was also an elected official—lost her reelection campaign by seventy-two votes. What a major disaster. For five years, I had worked tirelessly in the New York City Council and went from making $24,000 to over $100,000 annual salary. At the age of twenty-four, I had already bought my first home, had two cars, and was living what I considered to be the "baller's lifestyle." Think about it, what single person do you know has two cars—one to drive during the week and the other on the weekends? It made no sense, but that was the flamboyant lifestyle I created for myself. During my tenure at the City Council, I became the local bank for many of my friends and family. Everyone knew that when attending social events, the bill was on me. Losing both of these campaigns was totally unexpected, and I had no backup plan. In my eyes, everything I had worked for was abruptly coming to an end. Fearful, confused, and absolutely petrified, I didn't know where to turn or what to do. It was certainly the attack of the setbacks.

Your Adversity Is Your Advantage

My unexpected adversity was certainly challenging for me. I had to figure out how I was going to make a living, pay my bills, and maintain the lifestyle that I had already created. Shortly thereafter, I had to give up the cars and discover ways to drastically reduce my expenses. Although the situation for me seemed like a tragedy, it was a Blessing in disguise. The situation forced me to be humble and realign my values. At the lowest point of my life, I decided that I would never depend on just one stream of income again. In addition to this decision, I also redirected the efforts and energy that I gave to working for someone else to building my own businesses and empowering the masses to find and follow their own dreams. The adversity created the opportunity for me to be more resourceful and less boastful. It forced me to find myself and build my character. The adversity eventually became my advantage. Today, I'm a better man as a result of my adverse experience.

The Impact of a Setback

Author Willie Jolley is known for the saying, "A setback is a setup for a comeback." This quote gives perspective on how one should view obstacles. It's a statement of courage, resilience, and a progressive attitude. People who overcome Dreamicide are not impervious or immune to setbacks; they just view and respond to setbacks differently. How do you view and respond to your setbacks? The ways in which you handle setbacks are the building blocks of your character.

For every moment of glory in a person's life there is a background story. The stories are what make the person intriguing and inspiring. We admire leaders, sports figures, and entertainers, not just for what they've accomplished but also for what they've overcome. Oprah Winfrey was sexually abused as a child, she was demoted from her job as a news anchor, and was told that she wasn't fit for television. She now owns the Oprah Winfrey Network. Michael Jordan was cut from his high school basketball team but is now regarded in many circles as the GOAT (Greatest of All Time) in the game of basketball. Walt Disney was told he that he lacked imagination and had no original ideas, yet, every child's dream is to travel to Disney World. Tyler Perry's first play failed six times, and he eventually became homeless, but millions of people around the world now view his TV shows, movies, and other productions. Bishop T.D. Jakes had a lisp, considered to be a speech impediment. He was expected to fail as a pastor, but Jakes is now revered as one of America's greatest preachers. The list goes on and on.

We hear about these Success stories and the themes are similar, from pain to perseverance, from destruction to construction, from setbacks to comebacks. We often are mesmerized by their journeys, yet, when it relates to our goals, aspirations, and dreams, we hope for great results to come easily. If you want to be remembered like the greats while living your dreams, here is what you must accept: they don't build statues for people who cry, complain, and quit; they build statues for people who conquer and commit. Commit to the comeback; commit to your dreams. Your dreams will face setbacks, but if you expect the unexpected, you will overcome. In preparation for the potential setbacks that you may face, your dream will benefit from establishing your dream's S.O.S.

S.O.S.?

S.O.S. is widely known as the international sign of distress signal. It is used to alert authorities of emergency situations. In this chapter, S.O.S. is being used metaphorically in relation to your dreams. Often when my coaching clients express their fears of moving forward on their ideas, I have them create what I call a Setback Operating System (S.O.S.). This is a planning tool used to determine how they would stabilize themselves in the event that unexpected setbacks occur. It's really a worst-case scenario emergency plan for your dreams.

Developing Your S.O.S.

To develop your S.O.S., you will begin by clearly defining your desired outcome. Whether it's transitioning from your current job, moving to a new country, having a baby, or losing weight, the more specific you are, the greater the probability of ensuring a realistic plan in preparing your S.O.S. It might be helpful to use the Self Authored dreams that you recently created in Chapter 6. After clarifying your desired outcome, you will need to engage in what I call setback forecasting. Setback forecasting is making predictions about potential worst-case scenarios that could happen as you're pursuing your dreams. Again, be very specific. In the event that these setbacks occur, how would you stabilize yourself, keep your basic standard of living intact, and keep your dreams alive? A well, developed S.O.S. plan will help you overcome some of the anxieties you may experience due to these setbacks. If you know ahead of time what to do when setbacks strike, you will feel more comfortable pursuing your dreams despite these potential challenges. On the opposite page you'll find a sample S.O.S.

Your S.O.S. is what I consider to be the answer to "What's the worst that could happen?" If you anticipate the worst but work for the best, you will certainly find a level of peace of mind that allows you to clearly focus on total execution. Your dreams don't need a backup plan—you need a S.O.S.

SAMPLE S.O.S. PLAN

Setback Forecast

• Within a year, establish my portfolio and begin selling my artwork on etsy, ebay and other online retail platforms.

•Create my website to offer my artwork.

• Become more well known as an artist locally.

Desired outcome

• Due to unforeseen circumstances being unable to create enough art pieces for a comprehensive portfolio of professional quality.

• Family emergency depletes funds that were intended to pay for website.

• In lieu of having a completed portfolio, begin selling individual pieces through online platforms and using local venues for art exhibitions.

• Increase promotion of my art through a landing page and social media campaigns.

Setback Operating System

SUMMARY TAKEAWAYS

Setbacks are inevitable

» Don't take it personally—everyone experiences setbacks. Your passion will be the fuel to your persistence in these situations. Your setbacks are not stumbling blocks to progress—they are stepping stones to greatness.

The Adversity Advantage

» Adversity provides you with critical intelligence. It teaches you about your strengths and ability to overcome. Don't be imprisoned by adversity—it's a life lesson, not a life sentence. Your ability to overcome will serve to be advantageous especially when you are under pressure.

WHAT'S NEXT?

» Using the S.O.S. example on page 97, create your own S.O.S. Be sure to activate it in the event that your setbacks attack.

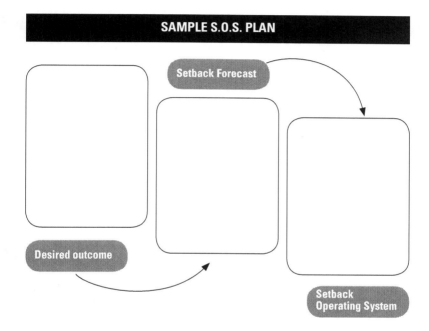

SAMPLE S.O.S. PLAN

Setback Forecast

Desired outcome

Setback Operating System

DREAM SUPPORT: BUILDING YOUR DREAM TEAM

Teamwork makes the dream work, but
a vision becomes a nightmare when the
leader has a big dream and a bad team.
—JOHN C. MAXWELL

Whoever walks with the wise becomes wise,
but the companion of fools will suffer harm.
PROVERBS 13:20 ESV

The year 1992 was undoubtedly a transformational one for the game of basketball. People from around the world were stunned by the performance of a team that many considered to be one of the greatest teams ever, in any sport. This was the year of the original Dream Team. Assembled for the Summer Olympics in Barcelona, the Dream Team was a phenomenon on and off the court. It didn't matter that they dominated the Olympic competition, beating their opponents by an average of forty-four points. What was fascinating was how this Dream Team gave fans a glimpse of basketball at its finest. The team included Michael Jordan, Earvin "Magic" Johnson, Larry Bird, and Charles Barkley, just to name a few. If you know anything about the game of basketball, you could clearly see why this team was unstoppable. Just search for these names in Google, and the statistics will speak for themselves.

What Made the Dream Team Powerful?

Beyond the enormous talent that was assembled to make this team possible, the Dream Team was effective because the entire team was committed to a common purpose. They knew their specific roles and were willing to put aside their competitive rivalries to support the collective mission of the team. Although the combination of talented players was impeccable, I would argue that their game-changing success wouldn't have been possible without the people that surveyed, supported, and surrounded the team. These aren't the people you often hear about. It's customary in sports, business, politics, and life in general to hear about the stars, without really knowing the people behind the stars. In the case of the Dream Team, those people were head coach Chuck Daly; assistant coaches Mike Krzyzewski, Lenny Wilkens, and P.J. Carlesimo; trainer Ed Lacerte; and team doctor David Fischer. In essence, the Dream Team was supported and surrounded by the right people, who were in the right place, for the right purpose—that was the power of the Dream Team.

Developing Your Dream Team

So, how is the story of the original US Olympic Dream Team relevant to you? I would suggest that if you want your dreams to live and flourish, your dreams also need the right people aligned strategically to fulfill your purpose. The problem with people who commit Dreamicide is that when situations become difficult, they seldom have a support structure of advisors to guide them through the challenges they face. In fact, your dreams might be surrounded with toxic individuals who are satisfied with you remaining stagnant. *Victims of Dreamicide often have people in their circle who are actually rooting for their demise.*

Take a moment and ask yourself: Who is in your circle? Who do you have supporting your vision? Do you currently have a powerful Dream Team? If not, it's essential that you build one. The greatest power that you have comes from the fact that you are the organizer of Your Dream's Destiny. You have the ability to decide who makes up your team and what roles they will play. Don't let the immediate comfort of your circle cause you to live the rest of your life uncomfortably. Whenever progress is being made, some folks will be left behind. If you can't change the mindset of the people around you, sometimes you just have to change the people who are around you. But if you feel unsettled about this concept of leaving folks behind, then look at it from this perspective: You didn't leave them behind—you just left them where they were comfortable. And you weren't comfortable with mediocrity.

The Mathematical Equation of Your Circle

I remember hearing one of my undergraduate professors say that everyone you know is a part of the mathematical equation of your life. Some people add and multiply, while others subtract and divide. The people who add value to your life help you to multiply your talents in pursuit of your dreams. People who subtract value from your life divide you from every dream that is important to you. The goal should be to spend more time with the adders and multipliers, while reducing or eliminating those who subtract and divide. Applying this principle will ensure that you avoid having negative integers in the sum of your equation.

Dream Assets vs. Dream Liabilities

Everyone who consumes your time and thoughts, or influences your actions is either an asset or liability. No one is neutral. The mere fact that they occupy your time will either add and multiply value, or subtract and divide from it.

Dream Assets

Adders and Multipliers are what I call your Dream Assets. These people understand your vision and are supportive towards your achievements. Your Assets have a vested interest in your growth. The Dream Asset is the person who is completely honest, respectful, and committed to helping you accomplish your dreams. As long as someone supports your vision, whether you've known him or her for ten days or ten years, they become an Asset to your life. If you want your dream to experience explosive growth, you will need four types of Assets. I call them, collectively, C4—a Confidant, Coach, Connector, and Confronter.

The Confidant

Your Confidants are the people with whom you can share any of your thoughts and feelings, without the fear of being judged. You can trust them with the information that you give. They will play a huge role in building your confidence. I personally only have a handful of Confidants, but my wife, Shereece, has by far been my greatest Dream Asset. Sheerece accepts my past, supports my present, and encourages my future. One of Shereece's greatest attributes is her ability to be honest but encouraging at the same time. I remember moments when I was too lazy to work on the manuscript for this book or prepare for a presentation. She would ask me, "Is this what you call Aiming High? What if your supporters knew that you were going back to sleep?" Although, it was frustrating at times, her words would whip me back into action. I am assured that whenever she speaks, it's never to break me down but always to build me up. A true Confidant is there for you regardless of the outcome. Every new thought, idea, or action is shared with Shereece privately, before it happens publicly. She doesn't always agree with me, but she certainly understands me. A hallmark of a great Confidant is his or her ability to exercise empathy.

The Coach

Your Coach is the person who will help you achieve your goals and/or improve your results. The Coach helps you to develop your specific, measurable performance outcomes. Your Coach should be able to provide guidance to you. They will have the ability to correct you without causing resentment. In some instances, these individuals may have already traveled on the path that you are pursuing. Your Coach will help you to "step your game up." Michael Jordan, one of the original Dream Team players, was good on the court, but when Phil Jackson became his coach, Michael Jordan became one of the greatest players of all time.

I personally still have Coaches to this day. Some with whom I've had long-term relationships and others that I've paid to coach me in specific areas. Yes, I've paid people to coach me; the investment in myself was certainly worth it, and I encourage others to find great Coaches, even if an investment is required. Think of it this way, losing weight on your own is possible, but paying for a professional personal trainer who specializes in fitness could expedite your results—if you follow the instructions. Even when you find a Coach, you have to be coachable as well. Your Coach at times may push you to uncomfortable levels to pull the best out of you. Try not to run away from the stretching that will occur. A Coach is only as good as the student taking the guidance. If you're not coachable, having a Coach has no value.

The Connector

Your Connector is the person who has relationships with or connections to the people, organizations, and resources that you need. They will be important in helping to expand your network. There are people who you may have encountered via different social events who already have the exposure, preparation, and access to circles to which you may not be connected. According to the Bureau of Labor Statistics, over 70 percent of jobs were filled due to a connection to someone in the workplace. Understanding this statistic reminds us of the old adage, it's not what you know, but who you know. Networking is essential to finding your connections. You may need to attend events related to your area of interest to eventually meet the right people who will connect you to your dreams. It's important that you identify your connectors and also make sure that you can reciprocate the value that you receive from them by being willing to share your connections as well. Always think of ways to add value to the people to whom you're connected.

The Confronter

Your Confronter is the person who will be unfiltered in their constructive feedback to you. They will challenge your thoughts, intentions, and actions. They will confront you when you attempt to make excuses. The Confronter is essential and must be given permission to be completely unfiltered and honest in providing you with feedback. At times, you will find yourself becoming frustrated towards your Confronter, but the ability to endure the confrontation will eventually make you stronger.

You have to be very careful in choosing your designated Confronter. You want to identify someone who can give you constructive feedback. It would be difficult to gain constructive feedback from someone who has never constructed anything. Your Confronter doesn't have to be directly involved in your area of interest, but they should be someone who has proven their ability to perform and get results in their respective field. As standard practice, I try not to take much advice from people I'm not willing to trade places with in any aspect of their lives.

Do You Have the C4?

Examine your circle and determine into which category the people in your life would fit. Do you have these types of Assets in your circle? Take a moment and reflect on this point, and write down at least one person who is serving in each category, below.

C4	NAME
Confidant	_____
Coach	_____
Connector	_____
Confronter	_____

Dream Liabilities

On the other end of the pendulum, you will find those who Subtract and Divide, or what I call your Dream Liabilities. All they do is cost you time and energy while leaving you in complete deficit. They point out what won't work as it relates to your dreams, as opposed to what could work. A Dream Liability has no problem encouraging you to compromise your dreams and aspirations, while they participate with you in activities that divert your attention from your mission.

We all know that person in our life with whom we may be spending much time, yet, we miss out on opportunities to make real progress. Keep in mind, someone who is a Dream Liability depends on you to remain at the same level to justify their failures, or lack of progress. What do I mean? Well, when you are making progress, there will be moments when people in your current circle might feel like they're failing if they aren't moving up themselves. They measure their success by comparing their current situation to the status of others. Someone who is a Dream Liability isn't very considerate of your time. They are leeches, and after they suck all the energy from you, they move on to the next source of energy. They bring a different type of C4; their explosives actually kill your dreams. Dream Liabilities take up countless hours of your time Complaining, Condemning, Confusing and Coveting.

As common practice, Overcomers of Dreamicide minimize the time spent discussing or focusing on these types of people. For purposes of giving you the ability to identify them, I will provide you with a brief description of who they are and what they spend the majority of their time doing.

Complaining—People who often express dissatisfaction or annoyance about a state of affairs or an event. They find problems with the past, present, and future.

Condemning—People who often express complete disapproval of what you're currently doing or hoping to accomplish.

Confusing—People who tend to cause confusion and chaos around you.

Coveting—People who constantly express a desire to have what belongs to you, eventually leading to envy and jealousy.

Surrounding yourself with people who are Dream Liabilities will always leave you at a loss. It would greatly benefit you to avoid their presence altogether.

Your Significant Other (Do Not Skip this Section)

Indulge me for a moment. I'm in no way claiming to be a relationship expert, but I have personally had a great deal of relationship experience that allows me to speak competently on this topic. The most important Dream Team decision you will make is who you choose as your partner. I strongly suggest you take your time in choosing a significant other that will be an asset to your dreams. One of the biggest mistakes you can make is being intimately involved with someone who is a significant liability. *You have to count the cost of your relationship. Anyone that costs you your dreams or peace of mind is too expensive to be around.* I've heard so many stories of people who gave up on their dreams because their significant other literally gave them more rope to hang their dreams. I can't stress this enough: do not waste time courting or dating a potential significant other who does not support your vision. He or she will become your greatest liability. Your dream will already endure many battles on the outside; you shouldn't have to go home to another round of continuous jabs, right hooks, and upper cuts that will totally knock out your dreams. Never forget that walking away from something or someone that is unhealthy is an act of bravery, even if you stumble on the way out the door.

SUMMARY TAKEAWAYS

Your Dream Team

» Your dream needs a team for it to flourish. Finding the right Confidant, Coach, Connector, and Confronter is essential to your growth. You must also get rid of people who often Complain, Condemn, Confuse and Covet.

Don't apologize for progress

» You owe no one an explanation as to why you've decided to make progress. Don't allow anyone to guilt you to mediocrity. Let go of those who are not assets to you. Choose Assets over Liabilities.

You are the sum of your circle

» You become who you spend the most time with. If you hang with four broke people, it's because you're the fifth broke person. Likewise, if four wealthy people surrounded you, you will become the fifth wealthy individual.

WHAT'S NEXT?

» Assess your circle and identify the people in your life who are Adders and Multipliers versus those who are Subtractors and Dividers. Add names to this list and act accordingly based on the recommendations given in this chapter.

YOUR CIRCLE OF INFLUENCE

ADDERS / MULTIPLIERS	SUBTRACTORS / DIVIDERS
1.	1.
2.	2.
3.	3.
4.	4.

SECTION III

met·rics
metriks/

noun
noun: **metrics**; *plural noun:* **metricses**

Standards of measurement by which
efficiency, performance, progress, or quality of a
plan, process, or product can be assessed.

THE OVERCOMERS METRICS

*Small gains lead to huge victories. When measuring
success, consistency is greater than intensity. Everyone
loves the home run, but more games are won by base
hits. If you focus your energy on consistently making
progress, over time your goals are sure to be reached.*

9

MEASURING SUCCESS: DO YOU HAVE KPIs?

If you can't measure it, you can't manage it.
—PETER DRUCKER

Let each one examine his own work.
Then he can take pride in himself and not
compare himself with someone else.

GALATIANS 6:4 NET

Legendary radio personality, speaker, and author Earl Nightingale, gave us a simple but profound definition of Success. In his book *The Strangest Secret*, he defined success as the progressive realization of a worthy ideal. This simply means that as long as you've created a worthy ideal and are consistently making progress towards it, you are achieving success. The only requirement is that it must be your "own" worthy ideal. If you desired to become a teacher, as long as you're making progress towards becoming a teacher, you are successful. Earl Nightingale's definition of success wouldn't be applicable if your decision to pursue the teaching profession was primarily or solely based on your parents', friends', or anyone else's desire for you to choose this career path. You must have internally desired to become a teacher. He didn't even say you had to achieve it yet; he merely stated that you have to be progressing towards it. This, for me, was quite an enlightening point of view.

Working for the Prize

I remember first hearing Earl Nightingale's definition; it totally changed my perspective and mindset related to how I measured success. We often get so focused on the prize we're trying to achieve, while failing to realize that the process is the prize in itself. What do I mean? Let's imagine you're in graduate school working towards earning a master's degree. Let's assume no one pressured you into attending graduate school; you're doing it because it's your worthy ideal. You believe earning the degree will put you in a much better position personally, professionally, and financially. So you wake up every day to sit in the classes, study the textbooks, and submit the assignments. Why are you doing this? To obtain the degree, right? Well, this process happens for approximately three years and then graduation day arrives. You walk the stage and receive your master's degree.

Was it a success? Most people would argue yes, because you achieved the goal—you earned the degree. So what happens now? The degree is placed in your office or on a wall in your home as a symbol of your hard work. Are you telling me that you worked so diligently over the three-year period to receive a sheet of paper? If your answer is yes, you could've saved so much money and avoided incurring student loan debt if you had just gone to Staples and typed the paper yourself. It wouldn't have been official, but you would've had your prize. You see, the prize isn't the degree. The prize was the late-night studying that helped you learn the importance of diligence. The prize was going to class consistently, which developed discipline. The prize was sacrificing partying with friends, or getting more hours of sleep, which allowed you to exercise determination. The prize isn't what you get; it's who you become. The prize is the process; the prize is your progress.

Are You Making Progress?

The ultimate measure of your success is whether or not you are making progress. The steps taken toward accomplishing your goals are your dominant measures. Are you consistently making the calls to your prospects? Are you finding ways to improve your presentation? Are you sticking to the weekly workout schedule at the gym? Are you constantly enhancing the value of your business? Although these tasks are not the glamorous end results, they are the necessary building blocks. Your dreams won't have operations without administration. All the small tasks, when executed consistently, are measures of progress. Stop beating up yourself because you haven't reached the mark yet. Success is a journey—not a destination. Small steps lead to big results, but if you quit because you're discouraged over the fact that you haven't made it to your end point, you will never get there. Do you remember the guy who quit the 2012 Olympics? Do you have any idea to whom I'm referring? You know who I'm talking about, right? The short guy who was very fast, but he quit the hundred-meter track race? What's his name again? Exactly my point; you don't remember if a quitter even exists, because we never remember the people who quit. Become the quitter and you'll be easily forgotten. Don't despise your humble beginnings. As the Chinese proverb says, "A journey of a thousand miles begins with a single step." Keep moving forward, and from today onward, you should focus your efforts on tracking your progress, not rehashing your problems.

Tracking Your Progress: Do You Know Your KPIs?

One afternoon while listening to the replay of a podcast on entrepreneurship, the host used a term that was totally unfamiliar to me. As an entrepreneur myself, the discussion made me very uncomfortable, as he kept on repeating the acronym. He said, "You have to know your KPIs. Your KPIs are everything. Without your KPIs, you're not in business." I asked myself, what in the world are KPIs, and why don't I know or have them? I immediately researched the terminology and found that KPI is an acronym for Key Performance Indicators. In business, the term is used to define the important measures of your businesses performance. KPIs are measurable values that demonstrate how effectively a company is achieving key objectives. Organizations use KPIs to evaluate their success at reaching targets. According to the Advanced Performance Institute, well-designed KPIs provide the vital navigation that helps us understand our current levels of performance.

Pardon the extensive business jargon, but here is my point—KPIs are essential not only to businesses but also for you and your dreams.

We All Need KPIs

Reflecting on this term, I think it's imperative that we all have KPIs. Knowing your KPIs will help you make educated decisions as they relate to how you move forward. They will help you to track your progress and know if you're growing, shrinking, or remaining stagnant. Tracking the progress on your KPIs will also help you determine whether, or not it's the right time to make major moves.

Ready to Resign?

In late 2016, a very good friend of mine was trying to determine whether or not he should leave his job. Over a ten-year period, he worked for a company in their sales department and was responsible for meeting yearly quotas. Deep inside, he felt that he could do better financially for himself if he transitioned and started his own business. However, he was fearful of making a move that could potentially jeopardize the stability of his family. He asked my opinion. I suggested that he develop KPIs to determine if he could really generate, on his own, what he was earning through his annual salary. The plan would be to set new personal quotas above the company's stated mandates and work diligently to meet those quotas. If he had the ability to surpass his job's quotas for six consecutive months, he could save the commissions earned to take care of his monthly living expenses. This would ultimately be an indicator to him that he could really do this on his own.

He worked the plan and made it happen. Month after month, he surpassed the company's expectations. He was on fire, and the company loved it. He continued to save the extra commissions in the process. Well, guess what? One year later, he left his job and has been in business for himself ever since.

The story of my friend is anecdotal, but it's indicative of what can happen when you know your KPIs. His decision to resign from his job was a hard one, but he became more confident when he was clear about what he was measuring.

As you pursue your dreams, you will need to know your own KPIs. To assist you in defining them, I believe you need to know and develop your KPIs in three primary areas to proceed with clarity. You need to understand Industry KPIs, Personal KPIs and Universal KPIs to set benchmarks and measure the growth of your dreams.

Industry KPIs

Every industry has KPIs. Let's take health care for example. If a doctor wants to determine whether or not a patient is healthy, instead of measuring random things, the doctor would focus on key health measures such as body mass index, cholesterol levels, blood pressure, and sugar levels. These are standard measures of an individual's health across the board.

No matter what industry your dreams fall into, there are key measures that are relative to how people operate in the industry. We usually define these as industry standards—a set of criteria relating to the standard functioning and carrying out of operations in a respective field. In other words, it is the generally accepted requirements followed by the members of an industry.

What are the widely accepted basic measures for your dream's industry? Knowing the basic measures provides you with the prerequisites that must be met to be in the game.

In any industry, the most effective KPIs are closely tied to specific objectives. A good starting point is therefore to develop KPQs—Key Performance Questions. At a minimum, what are the most widely accepted standards of performance for people or organizations in your industry? For example, back in the day, standard definition used to be widely acceptable for manufacturers of televisions, but today high definition television has become the norm. If you were in the TV-manufacturing industry, it would be wise for you to provide high definition capabilities in the production of all your televisions. Once the most important KPQs have been developed, it then allows you to select or develop the right KPIs that best help you to meet the standards. It would be highly beneficial for you to research your industries KPIs.

Let me pause here momentarily, as I speak about KPIs, you may be saying, "Sherman, my dreams have nothing to do with business." And I hear you; I'm using business as an example.

Let's say your dreams were related to building a better relationship with your family. Your KPIs may be related to the basic amount of activities or hours you want to spend with your family on a monthly basis. The main point of what I'm saying is that you have to be very specific about what your KPIs look like for your dreams. Now let's move on.

Personal KPIs

While understanding the industry is important, you should also commit yourself to meeting or surpassing the basic industry standards for your dreams. Whether or not you have the ability or resources to do so, it's imperative that you also develop your own Personal KPIs. Personal KPIs are unique to your personal values. At a minimum, what are the basic standards of performance that you will provide quantitatively and qualitatively? As an empowerment speaker and personal growth consultant, my basic standard of performance is to always give more than expected. I measure my progress with my clients by ensuring that I always overdeliver. It's about ensuring that I don't allow my ego to write checks that my character can't cash. Exceeding expectations is what allows me to have repeat clients for my speaking engagements and consulting contracts. Values such as honesty, integrity, consistency, and excellence are the cornerstone of my Personal KPIs. Your personal KPIs have to be set by you and not be based on comparisons to anyone else. Develop your personal KPIs based on your personal values and standards.

Universal KPIs

Beyond the Industry and Personal KPIs, I believe there are Universal KPIs that are applicable to everyone. Often when we measure progress, it's easy to look for data on sales, revenue and overall income to determine performance. As a matter of fact, it's no surprise that one of the biggest reasons why people allow their dreams to die is because they lose hope in the belief that their passion could produce profits. Personally, I disagree with this school of thought. Here's the fact: money will never make your passion, but your passion could always make you money. If people can make a living and become millionaires selling painted rocks, then you cannot convince me that a person's passion can't generate income. The reason why your passion might not be producing profits is because you have not yet answered three important questions.

1. What do you find easy and natural to do that others may find difficult? (Your passion or gift is within what you naturally do.)
2. What could you enjoy doing everyday of your life, without having to get paid for it? (Your passion lies within what you are able to consistently enjoy without needing a monetary reward.)
3. How could your deep inner passion impact society? (Your passion could produce profits if you figure out how it contributes to people's lives.)

The Value of Your Presence

The value of your life will not be measured by the materials you acquire but by the people you empower. You empower people through your service. Therefore, universally if you begin to focus on how your service could have greater Impact, this will give you Influence and eventually generate Income. Most people try it the other way around; they focus on Income, to have Impact and Influence. My suggestion is that you start with IMPACT.

Impact

Impact is the most important universal KPI. Without impact, everything you do is insignificant. When measuring your performance you need to measure your Impact. Are you positively impacting the bottom line of a company? Are you positively impacting people emotionally, socially, or economically? Are you positively improving the standards of living or quality of life for people? If your presence is not having a positive Impact, you won't gain positive profits from your passion. If Impact is a key measure of your progress, you will be forced to continually question how your presence consistently adds value and Impacts your environment.

Influence

Influence is a universal measure of your performance. The more Impact you have the more Influence you will gain. People with Influence are greatly admired and looked to for advice and guidance. In the current social media driven landscape, organizations, and people are aligning themselves with Influencers. People who have great Impact garner more Influence, because they've exercised a proven ability to affect the thoughts, behaviors, and feelings of others. If your passion and presence has great influence, people and organizations are often willing to find ways to meet your needs, so that they in turn may benefit from the value of your time. Your Influence is a reflection of your Impact.

Income

Income is a by-product of Impact and Influence. It is the least important Universal KPI. We often see celebrities, moguls, and great influencers generate huge amounts of Income, even when they don't need it because of their Impact and Influence. If you focus too much on Income, you may find yourself making decisions that are expedient in making a quick buck, while possibly compromising the value of your long-term impact. Don't get me wrong, money is important for all that we do, but if it becomes the primary focus, we will never experience the long-term bonuses that only come from having authentic impact. If you want to generate more Income, find ways to have more Impact, then invest the profits back into having greater Impact and this cycle will continually allow you to expand.

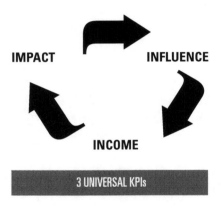

Your Progress = Your Legacy

When Abraham Maslow created what is known as Maslow's hierarchy of needs, the highest need in his hierarchy was the need for Self-actualization. Self-actualization is defined as realizing personal potential and self-fulfillment by seeking personal growth and peak experiences. One can never be totally fulfilled by external results. Therefore, on the quest for self-actualization you have to know that your progress is your self-actualized legacy. Your legacy is not about what you leave behind for people, but what you leave within the people that you've impacted. The ultimate measure is whether the world will experience the feeling of presence in the midst of your absence. What's important is not what you had, but what you did. During your life, did you make progress? Did you leave a legacy? Take these words to heart—your legacy will be greater than your currency.

SUMMARY TAKEAWAYS

Progress is the prize

» Progress is the greatest factor that drives human pursuits. We live to grow, improve, and get better. Let the end results be a bonus, but make progress your focus.

Clarify your KPIs

» Your Key Performance Indicators will help you to track your progress. Every dream has industry-specific KPIs, but don't neglect to develop your personal KPIs and live by the Universal KPIs. Remember Impact increases Influence and generates Income.

Live your legacy

» Your life is your legacy. What you do will forever be etched into the history of the world. Live a life that is meaningful, impactful, and leave an indelible mark.

WHAT'S NEXT?

» Create a list of Industry KPIs, and examine whether or not you are meeting the basic industry standards. Develop your own Personal KPIs, and use these as your distinguishing attributes. Clearly articulate how your presence and what you do is making an Impact in the world.

WHAT ARE YOUR KPIs?

INDUSTRY KPIs	PERSONAL KPIs
1.	1.
2.	2.
3.	3.

10

THE DREAM GAP: BETWEEN NO LONGER AND NOT YET

Remember how far you've come, not just how far
you have to go. You are not where you want to
be, but neither are you where you used to be.

—RICK WARREN

But they who wait for the Lord shall renew
their strength; they shall mount up with
wings like eagles; they shall run and not be
weary; they shall walk and not faint.

ISAIAH 40:31 ESV

Even as I encourage you to aggressively pursue your goals, dreams, and aspirations, it's imperative that I also urge you to avoid becoming so overly consumed by the pursuit that you ultimately neglect to appreciate the process. There is a sacred space that should be respected and honored at all times. Appreciating this space is essential to ensuring that you live every moment with contentment, fulfillment, and peace of mind. This space is the gap that we continually attempt to close. It's a gap that we develop after reaching a milestone or achieving a goal. This pivotal gap is between the real and the ideal, a gap between what we have, and what we want; it's the gap between where we are and where we are going, the gap between no longer and not yet. This ever-present gap will always exist as long as we desire more from life. If not approached delicately, this gap could cause extreme misery. On the other hand, appreciating this gap could be a catalyst for life-sustaining happiness and joy. The key to honoring this space and using it to your advantage is to consistently remind yourself that you are closer today than you were yesterday.

You Are Closer than You Were

Take a moment and reflect on where you were before you arrived at where you are. I'm sure you can agree that something has changed. Before you drove a car, you were walking or taking the bus; before you got your job, you were praying and hoping to find employment. The gap between where you are now, and where you want to be was created as a result of your successful realization of a desired milestone. Now that you've arrived, you've created yet another level that you aspire to reach. Our human instinct will never allow us to be completely satisfied. The pursuit of growth keeps us alive and going. That's why it's said, if you're not growing, you're dying. When you truly appreciate the fact that you are progressing, you will spend less time feeling despondent about your current circumstances. No matter when and where you started the journey to your dreams, you are closer than where you were. At times it may not feel like it, and in other moments it won't look like it, but trust me when I say, you are closer. When climbing the mountain, it's easy to focus on how much farther you have travel, while forgetting to look back on how far you've come. Don't despise your humble beginnings; you have achieved some of the milestones you once wished for. I wouldn't be surprised to discover that our Creator sometimes won't give us what we ask for, just to avoid giving us something more to complain about. When you are in a space in which you no longer find delight with your present circumstance and are finally ready to leap toward your new aspiration, you are in the middle of your dream Gap.

Complaining about the Gap will not close it, crying about the Gap will not minimize it. You only want more because you have more. So it's incumbent upon you to learn how to appreciate the Gap.

Why Do We Desire More?

What we hope for in life is predominantly a function of where we are in life. We don't yearn or desire for what we've already acquired. Often our current possessions or positions diminish in value as soon as something new catches the eye. Take shoes for example: for the man who has no shoes, all he hopes for is one pair. But the man who has one pair desires a newer pair. The man who has a newer pair hopes for more pairs, while the man who has no feet only hopes for feet, so he can walk the earth barefooted. Again, what you want from life is always a function of where you are. Embrace the fact that even when you don't have much, you still have more than many. You should never let the things you want make you forget the things you have.

According to a 2013 article titled, "Poverty Facts and Stats," Anup Shah posited that "almost half the world—over three billion people—live on less than $2.50 per day. And at least 80 percent of humanity lives on less than $10 a day." Yet, all over the world, there are people who live fulfilled lives even while living in these conditions of extreme poverty. How is this accomplished? The people in these third world countries have figured out ways to survive in the midst of seemingly insurmountable odds. They don't have or see much, so they don't desire for much more than the basics, and they appreciate having little. While you find time to complain about your issues, someone in the world would love to have your problems. You only desire more because you have more—you have more than many. This perspective should impact you profoundly and serve as a reminder that you and I have lots to be grateful and appreciative for. Imagine, within the United States of America, a person could be at the lowest level of the poverty line and yet suffer from obesity. They might be considered suffering socioeconomically, but they are not starving physically. Other places don't have this luxury. Suffering and starving are one and the same. It's in your best interest to live your life with wholehearted appreciation, no matter the situation.

To Cancel Frustration, Begin with Appreciation

I was surprised when I read that the world's wealthiest countries often rank lowest in the happiness index. A study by the World Economic Forum in 2016 indicated that some of the happiest countries were not the wealthiest. Professor Jeffrey Sachs, one of the authors of this report, stated, "For a society that just chases money, we are chasing the wrong things. Our social fabric is deteriorating, social trust is deteriorating, faith in government is deteriorating." The report also stated "When countries single-mindedly pursue individual objectives, such as economic development to the neglect of social and environmental objectives, the results can be highly adverse for human wellbeing, even dangerous for survival." My friend, understand this: the most important things in life are not things; they're people. People will sometimes disappoint, discourage, or dissuade you from your dreams, but other people will enrich, enhance, and encourage you along the way. People are the only ones who can truly understand us. As long as we have people in our lives, good or bad, let's appreciate them. Your loved ones are important; they are the ones that you will think of the most before you die. Make it a point to spend most of your time in life with the people who will cry the most after your funeral. I think of my wife and daughter; my mother, father, and brother; my aunts and uncles; nieces and nephews. I think about those who were family to me although they weren't blood related. All of these people matter most. And people who matter most should never be at the mercy of things that matter least. Your dreams matter, but your loved ones matter more. I beg you that while you fight to keep your dreams alive, don't let it live at the expense of your loved ones— but together with your loved ones. Time is precious; make sure to use it wisely.

To cancel frustration, you must begin with appreciation. Appreciate the tough times, appreciate the fun times, appreciate the ups, and appreciate the downs. When you go to the hospital and they hook you up to a heart monitor, the lines are expected to go up and down. Because if you ever flatline, it means you're dead. So if you find yourself going through the ups and downs in pursuit of your dream, remember that as long as you have life, you have much to be grateful for. I conclude, by sharing the words that I've shared with thousands of people who've heard my messages all around the world, and now I share with you.

> *As the world turns, you will go through pain and*
> *struggle,*
> *But still juggle with the hope of being successful*
> *tomorrow,*
> *Some think you will not make it, but they are sadly*
> *mistaken,*
> *Your Journey has just begun and you're quickly*
> *accelerating,*
> *To higher heights, with a vision beyond sight.*
> *So bright that many are blinded by your light,*

You're a shining star and you are destined to win,
You're Overcoming Dreamicide, keep doing your
thing,
And as you do it, be sure to rebuke all negativity,
Take steps forward and make your dreams a
reality.

Look, I appreciate you. If you haven't found anyone else who believes in you, trust and know that I do. Go out there and conquer the world, but first begin by conquering with your family and at your home. Let's keep on pushing, progressing, and fighting to make things happen for our families, for our loved ones, for our legacy. This is Sherman Browne, reminding you to never let the dreams die—keep your dreams alive. Together on this journey we are Overcoming Dreamicide!

ACKNOWLEDGMENTS

To **Riley Gray**: You are the unseen force behind the AIMHigh movement and my personal brand. Thank you for always challenging me and never doubting the vision!

To the **Wright Family**: They say blood is thicker than water, but water is needed to survive. Thank you for the inseparable bond between our families and for helping to shape my thought process in preparation for this book.

To **Cordell Boynes and Jason Sorhaindo**: We grew and conquered together; your support in all my endeavors has never been taken for granted.

To my unfiltered constructive critics: **Tishma de Lagarde and Denise Senderson**, thank you for always being brutally honest and for your prompt responses whenever feedback was needed.

To the members of the **AIMHigh Empowerment Institute**: Thank you all for allowing me to live my dream #AIMHighEI. Special thanks to our chairman and my evaluator, **Andre Samuels**.

To **Patrice Francois, Kevin "Moon" Claxton, and Janillia Seraphin**: Thank you for readily recognizing what you considered to be my Power Quotes.

To my accountability group, **"Win 17"**: Our four-month encounter made this book so much stronger. Special thanks to **Crystal Camejo**, for keeping our group together and keeping me accountable to my deadlines.

To my power prayer warriors **Michele Rodney** and **Miriam Edwards:** Thank you for always challenging me and allowing me to share my trials and triumphs with you. When in doubt, I knew your prayers were there.

To my pastor, **Rev. Devon Dixon**, and **First Lady Heather Dixon:** Thank you for being a true example of what it means to be Genuine People of God.

BIBLIOGRAPHY

Introduction

Janiszewski, Peter. "The Science of Starvation: How long can humans survive without food or water?" *Obesity Panacea, PLOS.org* (blog), (May, 13, 2011). blogs.plos.org/obesitypanacea/2011/05/13/the-science-of-starvation-how-long-can-humans-survive-without-food-or-water/.

Definition of "-cide" from Dictionary.com. www.dictionary.com/browse/-cide. Accessed Sep. 10, 2017.

Section I

Definition of "mindset" from Dictionary.com. www.dictionary.com/browse/mindset. Accessed Sep. 10, 2017.

Chapter 1

"30 Lessons for Living" author Karl A. Pillemer shares life lessons from older Americans (2012) live.washingtonpost.com/30-lessons-for-living.html.

Pillemer, Karl. "When people look back on their lives, what are common regrets they have? Of those regrets, how many are based on false assumptions or premises?" Quora.com (Oct. 28, 2014). www.quora.com/When-people-look-back-on-their-lives-what-are-common-regrets-they-have/answer/Karl-Pillemer?srid=J7c3&share=1.

"Researchers confirm that 'YOLO' is sound life advice." (n.d.) www.washingtonpost.com/news/wonk/wp/2017/02/28/researchers-confirm-that-yolo-is-sound-life-advice/?utm_term=.b99be94efc4f.

Elderman, Marian Wright. "Remembering Dr. Benjamin E Mays' Legacy." Huffpost. www.huffingtonpost.com/marian-wright-edelman /remembering-dr-benjamin-e_b_871139.html. June 3, 2011.

Martino, Joe. "Someone Asked the Dalai Lama What Surprises Him Most, His Response Was Mind Altering." Collective Evolution (website). www.collective-evolution.com/2014/05/25/someone-asked-the -dalai-lama-what-surprises-him-most-his-response-was-mind-altering/. May 25, 2014.

Chapter 2

Sisk, Richard. "South Bronx is poorest district in nation, U.S. Census Bureau finds: 38% live below poverty line. NY Daily News. www.ny dailynews.com/new-york/south-bronx-poorest-district-nation-u-s-census -bureau-finds-38-live-poverty-line-article-1.438344. Sep. 29, 2010.

Chapter 3

Blocker, Wayne. "Stages of Pregnancy: Week by Week." OnHealth (website). www.onhealth.com/content/1/pregnancy_stages_trimesters . June 21, 2016.

Smith, Scott S. "Grounds for Success: Coffee Talk with Starbucks CEO Howard Schultz." Entrepreneur.com. www.entrepreneur.com/article /15582. May 1, 1998.

Vinnedge, Mary. "Arianna Huffington: Pushing the Limits: How the Political Insider Turned Blogger Gained Courage from Failure." Success. com. www.success.com/article/arianna-huffington-pushing-the-limits. Sep. 19, 2010.

Volpe, Allie. "Q&A: Kevin Hart on 'mind-blowing' tour, chicken and Philly roots." *Inquirer.* www.philly.com/philly/blogs/entertainment /music_nightlife/QA-Kevin-Hart-on-mind-blowing-tour-chicken-and -Philly-roots-.html. Feb. 19, 2015.

"Joseph the Dreamer." Biblehub.com. biblehub.com/library/anonymous /children_of_the_old_testament/joseph_the_dreamer.htm. Accessed Sep. 10, 2017.

Chapter 4

Definition of "excusitis." CollinsDictionary.com. www.collinsdictionary
.com/us/submission/1345/EXCUSITIS. Accessed Sep. 10, 2017.

Section II

Definition of "method." Dictionary.com. www.dictionary.com/browse
/method. Accessed Sep. 10, 2017.

Chapter 5

Definition of "system." BusinessDictionary.com. www.businessdictionary
.com/definition/system.html. Accessed Sep. 10, 2017.

"Our History." McDonald's.com. www.mcdonalds.com/us/en-us/about-
us/our-history.html. Accessed Sep. 10, 2017.

Biz Privy Image (2016) me.me/i/instagram-the-most-valuable-photo
-company-sells-no-cameras-alibaba-4536473.

"Our Trip History." Uber.com. www.uber.com/our-story/. Accessed
Sep. 10, 2017.

Chapter 6

"Helen Keller." Biography.com. www.biography.com/people/helen-keller
-9361967. Last updated July 7, 2017.

"Vision Board." www.pinterest.com/secretvision/vision-board/.
Accessed Sep. 10, 2017.

Kamenetz, Anya. "Self Authoring: The Writing Assignment that
Changes Lives." www.npr.org/sections/ed/2015/07/10/419202925/the
-writing-assignment-that-changes-lives. July 10, 2015.

"What Oprah learned from Jim Carrey." Oprah's Life Class. Oprah.
com. www.oprah.com/oprahs-lifeclass/what-oprah-learned-from-jim
-carrey-video. Oct. 12, 2010.

Vaden, Rory. "The Focus Funnel." RoryVaden.com. roryvaden.com
/blog/the-focus-funnel/. May 13, 2015.

Chapter 7

"Famous Failures: Albert Einstein, Michael Jordan, Walt Disney, Steve Jobs, Oprah Winfrey, The Beatles." Inspiration in Pictures (website). www.inspirationinpictures.com/famous-failures/. May 13, 2013.

"Bishop T.D. Jakes." The History Makers (website). www.thehistory makers.com/biography/bishop-td-jakes-33. Aug 25, 2010.

Morris, Sophia. "Stars who were once homeless—Tyler Perry." Time. com. newsfeed.time.com/2013/07/11/stars-who-were-once-homeless /slide/tyler-perry/. July 11, 2013.

Chapter 8

"The Original Dream Team." NBA.com. www.nba.com/history/dreamT _moments.html. Accessed Sep. 10, 2017.

Section III

Definition of "metrics" from BusinessDictionary.com. www.business dictionary.com/definition/metrics.html. Accessed Sep. 10, 2017.

Chapter 9

Advanced Performance Institute, "What is a Key Performance Indicator" (2017). www.ap-institute.com/what-is-a-key-performance-indicator.

Chapter 10

Shah, Anup. "Poverty Facts and Stats." GlobalIssues.org (Last updated Jan. 7, 2013). www.globalissues.org/article/26/poverty-facts-and-stats.

Breene, Keith. "The world's happiest countries in 2016." World Economic Forum (Nov. 14, 2016). www.weforum.org/agenda/2016/11/the -worlds-happiest-countries-in-2016/.

@Shermanbrowne

CONNECT WITH SHERMAN

WWW.SHERMANBROWNE.COM

AIMHigh Ambassadors are a community of progressive thinkers, adventurers, achievers and life-changers. As a network of like-minded individuals from diverse socio-economic, academic, personal and professional backgrounds, Ambassadors are engaged, educated and empowered to activate their legacies and leave a lasting impact on the world.

Benefits of being an AIMHigh Ambassador

- Exclusive Access to Sherman Browne & AIMHigh resources and training.

- The ability to Network with a Community of Progressive Individuals

- Access to accountability partners via our Closed Facebook Group.

- Periodic conference calls for live Q & A related to your specific goals.

- Proven strategies and resources to move to a higher level.

SIGN UP NOW AT
www.shermanbrowne.com

AIMHigh Insights, is a weekly video series providing viewers with thought- provoking anecdotes, quotes, stories and systems for success to stimulate their Ambition, Inspiration, and Motivation (AIM). Sign up to have weekly videos delivered to your inbox.

"Find Your Purpose"

"Recognize Your Value"

"How To Take Action"

SUBSCRIBE TODAY!
www.Shermanbrowne.com

NO MAN LEFT BEHIND

www.aimhighei.org

Academically Focused. Life Skills Driven.

AIMHIGH
EMPOWERMENT INSTITUTE

WHO WE ARE:

We are a community of students, faculty, staff, alumni, graduate students and industry professionals who are committed to transforming the lives and shaping a better future for students from elementary school through college and beyond.

WHAT WE DO:

We provide rites of passage programming for cohorts of students to improve APPS (Academic, Personal, Professional and Social) outcomes. The goal is to dismantle the "School to Prison Pipeline" while establishing a new "School to Prominence model."

Our Measures

- We improve Attendance and Retention Rates.
- We Reduce Disciplinary Issues and Drop-Out Rates
- Overall we help to prevent Juvenile Delinquency
- We increase Grade Point Averages and Graduation Rates.

HOW WE DO IT:

Using our Epic Impact Formula $FeMC^2$, we work with students to develop both persistence and intelligence in education and life endeavors.

For more info email **info@aimhighei.org** or visit **www.aimhighei.org**

ABOUT THE AUTHOR

Sherman Browne's story demonstrates the results that come from being civically engaged, collegiately educated and conscientiously empowered. Raised in the U.S. Virgin Islands, in 2002 he migrated to New York City in pursuit of a career in the performing arts. While living in the Bronx, Sherman resided with his grandmother in the poorest congressional district of the United States. It was under these humble circumstances that he developed his guiding philosophy that "One should never allow their geography to be the author of their biography." Grieved by the conditions of his community, he decided to write a new story for his life by switching career paths to focus on community development and personal, economic and social empowerment.

To accomplish this feat, in 2004 Sherman served as a Community Liaison, Chief of Staff and later Senior Policy & Budget Advisor in the New York City Council where he helped secure over $60 Million in funding for education, affordable housing and sports / recreational programs. To increase civic participation in the Bronx, in 2007, Browne was unanimously appointed by the NYC Board of Commissioners to serve as Acting Deputy Chief Clerk for the Board of Elections. During this period he spearheaded the reorganization efforts to improve efficiency and effectiveness in the overall delivery of Bronx Board of Election services.

Sherman has earned a Bachelor's in Business Administration from Monroe College and a Master's in Public Administration from NYU. He is also an Adjunct Professor of Business, Criminal Justice and the Social Sciences. His commitment to empowering the masses is surpassed only by his Faith in God and dedication to his family as a loving husband to his wife Shereece Browne and their daughter Solaei Browne.

Made in the USA
Columbia, SC
11 January 2018